This Book

presented to the

CHURCH LIBRARY IN MEMORY OF

Harry Knight

BY

Birdville Baptist Church

Code 4386-23, No. 3, Broadman Supplies, Nashville, Tenn. Printed in USA

LAYMAN'S LIBRARY OF CHRISTIAN DOCTRINE

The Christian Hope

MORRIS ASHCRAFT

BROADMAN PRESS
Nashville, Tennessee

To

Mark and Anna

© Copyright 1988 • Broadman Press

All rights reserved

4216-45

ISBN: 0-8054-1645-5

Dewey Decimal Classification: 236

Subject Heading: ESCHATOLOGY

Library of Congress Catalog Card Number: 87-29998

Printed in the United States of America

Library of Congress Cataloging-in-Publication Data

Ashcraft, Morris.
  The Christian hope.

  (Layman's library of Christian doctrine ; 15)
  Includes index.
  1. Hope—Religious aspects—Christianity.   I. Title.
II. Series.
BV4638.A84   1988   236   87-29998
ISBN 0-8054-1645-5

Foreword

The *Layman's Library of Christian Doctrine* in sixteen volumes covers the major doctrines of the Christian faith.

To meet the needs of the lay reader, the *Library* is written in a popular style. Headings are used in each volume to help the reader understand which part of the doctrine is being dealt with. Technical terms, if necessary to the discussion, will be clearly defined.

The need for this series is evident. Christians need to have a theology of their own, not one handed to them by someone else. The *Library* is written to help readers evaluate and form their own beliefs based on the Bible and on clear and persuasive statements of historic Christian positions. The aim of the series is to help laymen hammer out their own personal theology.

The books range in size from 140 pages to 168 pages. Each volume deals with a major part of Christian doctrine. Although some overlap is unavoidable, each volume will stand on its own. A set of the sixteen-volume series will give a person a complete look at the major doctrines of the Christian church.

Each volume is personalized by its author. The author will show the vitality of Christian doctrines and their meaning for everyday life. Strong and fresh illustrations will hold the interest of the reader. At times the personal faith of the authors will be seen in illustrations from their own Christian pilgrimage.

Not all laymen are aware they are theologians. Many may believe they know nothing of theology. However, every person believes something. This series helps the layman to understand what he believes and to be able to be "prepared to make a defense to anyone who calls him to account for the hope that is in him" (1 Pet. 3:15, RSV).

Acknowledgments

While working on this volume, I taught a course in Christian Eschatology to the Associate of Divinity class of Southeastern Seminary. These students read the outlines, two chapters, and offered helpful criticisms of this study. I am grateful to them for their responses.

I am especially indebted to Ms. Cecelia Hensley for typing the manuscript, and to my research assistant Ms. Penny Godfrey for hours spent getting volumes from the library and in proofreading the final manuscript.

MORRIS ASHCRAFT
December 1986
Wake Forest, NC

Contents

1
What Is Hope?

A healthy human being lives every moment in three time zones: past, present, and future. Each of these adds a richness without which life would not be human. We know the past through memory and history. We know the present by observation, listening, and reflection. We participate in the future by anticipation—either dread or hope.

If a person is lacking in any of these areas we are alarmed. We call for help. If one cannot remember the past or is indifferent about it, something is amiss. If one cannot or will not perceive the present, we say that person is out of touch with reality, a very serious condition if it continues long. If a person has no hope, does not anticipate the future with some sense of purpose or goal, we know that despair and meaninglessness cast a dark cloud over that life and those related to it.

This book is about hope. We are interested in looking toward the future with anticipation, purpose, meaning, destiny. This hope draws heavily upon the past for guidance, bequeaths a lavish endowment to the present in numerous ways, and makes tomorrow a joyful adventure.

We speak of *Christian hope*. The term draws its meaning from Jesus Christ, His life, death, resurrection, and promises. Because of who He was and what He did, Christian hope brightens all tomorrows and beckons all of us to an ultimate reunion with all believers and with God with whom we expect to live eternally.

Hope as Christian Eschatology

Death appears to pose the most threatening question about the future. Some centuries before Christ came, Job worded the haunting question which has been voiced throughout the ages: "If a man die, shall he live again?" (Job 14:14). But, Job did not get a clear answer.

When Jesus Christ was raised from the dead, He gave the answer. Paul worded it as follows: "But in fact Christ has been raised from the dead, the first fruits of those who have fallen asleep. For as by a man came death, by a man has come also the resurrection of the dead. For as in Adam all die, so also in Christ shall all be made alive" (1 Cor. 15:20-22). Christian hope certainly includes the expectation of the resurrection, but much more.

Christians understand human existence as a continuous line starting at creation and ending in a consummation. That "end" is usually discussed under the title "Eschatology." The word was formed from two Greek words, *eschata* which means "last things" and *logia* which means "study of" or "science of."

Christian eschatology attempts to understand the major themes related to the "end." The subjects usually included are death, resurrection, life after death, the coming of Christ, the kingdom of God, judgment, heaven, and hell.

In this volume, I have chosen to discuss these eschatological themes under the heading of "Christian Hope." There are several reasons for this approach. *Hope* is a biblical word; *eschatology* is not. Hope is vitally related to other Christian themes, such as faith and love; eschatology can become so speculative that it may lose its personal nature. Hope ties together past, present, and future; eschatology tends to deal with only the future. Hope maintains a living relationship with life as we live it in relationship to the "end"; eschatology has been known to issue in an "otherworldliness" which seeks to escape life.

In this study, I use the word *hope* to include all of the themes which legitimately belong in an eschatology, but I shall attempt to maintain a personal and living relationship with these beliefs as they emerged in the early Christian communities and continued growing within them and us, even unto this day.

A Preliminary Definition of Hope

Hope is faith looking into the future. Christian hope is an expectation that God who has acted in past history and is active in our lives today will keep His promises tomorrow. It is the conviction that God will bring to a joyful conclusion that which He has begun for and within us.

Christian hope always has an orientation toward the future, but its basic character incorporates the past and the present.

Christian hope always has its foundation in Jesus Christ. The Christian hope emerged out of the life, teachings, death, and resurrection of Jesus. Peter's sermons at Pentecost (Acts 2—4) reflect the origin of Christian hope in these events with a special emphasis on the resurrection. Repentance leads to the forgiveness of sins in the name of Jesus Christ now, and there is "no other name under heaven given among men by which we must be saved" (Acts 4:12).

Jesus Christ is our hope. Paul related all Christian beliefs to Jesus Christ in such a way that he could write that Christ Jesus is "our hope" (1 Tim. 1:1).

The early Christians lived with a strong expectation that God would come to them soon. They had come to know Him through Christ so recently. They lived their days in the anticipation of Christ's return. Two of their earliest confessions were "Maranatha" and "Jesus is Lord."

The Aramaic word *Maranatha* may mean "Our Lord has come" or in Paul's conclusion to 1 Corinthians "Our Lord, come!" (16:22). The disciples used a similar expression, "The Lord is at hand" (Phil. 4:5).

The New Testament ends with the expression of this hope, "Come, Lord Jesus!" (Rev. 22:20).

Tensions and Dangers

In the study of Christian hope there are tensions and dangers which we must recognize.

Tension Between Individual Hope and Collective Hope

Christian hope includes many themes that are distinctively individual, such as death. Other themes are certainly collective or corporate, such as the kingdom of God. Others are either or both, such as resurrection and judgment. One can lapse into error easily if these distinctions are forgotten or misused.

Tension Between This World and the Next

Christians have on many occasions escaped the tension by withdrawing from this world in interest of the next world. This danger, while it may appear at the moment to be Christian, is in reality irresponsible. Hope for the next world does not result in escape from this one; rather, such hope strengthens a person for this earthly life.

The Danger of Exaggerated Emphasis on One Theme

Christian history tells us of many tragic events in which sincere believers became so obsessed with one aspect of Christian hope that they forgot all of the others. Millennial beliefs are the most obvious examples. When I was a child, I heard preachers who were so obsessed with the hope of "the second coming" that they forgot the other themes of hope.

The Danger of Giving Primary Attention to Secondary Issues

The great themes of Christian hope are the resurrection from the dead, the kingdom of God, the coming of Christ, the judgment, and the life everlasting. Millennial views are discussed appropriately in connection with the coming of Christ or the kingdom of God.

The Danger of All or Nothing

Under different pressures and in different ages, believers tend to emphasize one or more of the themes of hope and neglect the others. Other believers often insist that either we accept a particular eschatological belief or we reject all of them. We should not place others in this position or allow ourselves to be forced into such a choice. Some people think that the most important event at the end of history will be the establishment of a kingdom on earth. Others think that this will not happen or, if it does, that it is secondary to the larger theme. Some believers cringe at the thought of an intermediate state between individual death and final judgment. They want to go on to the full joys of heaven immediately. We need to recognize, however, that if we are with Christ that will be adequate whether it is an intermediate state or a final one, on earth or elsewhere.

A fuller definition of hope will emerge from the study of the biblical themes related to our future with God.

A Cardinal Christian Virtue

The Greek philosophers in their consideration of human ethics tended to stress four cardinal virtues: wisdom, courage, temperance, and justice. Paul extolled three cardinal virtues for Christians: faith, hope, and love. He concluded the great hymn on love, "So faith, hope, love abide, these three; but the greatest of these is love" (1 Cor. 13:13). To be sure, the greatest of these is love. But, the first of these is faith. And, standing between the two and holding them together is hope. Love never stands alone. Faith and hope are the constant companions of Christian love.

Faith has an anchor in the past. Faith, while very present in the life of today, looks back to the great events of revelation of which Jesus Christ is the central event. Love is the "God-kind" of love which is not motivated by value, response, or expected response. The love of Christ, which becomes a part of us, was such that He died for us (2 Cor. 5:14). This Christlike love reaches beyond human barriers and makes it possible for one to love one's enemies. Paul defined it in his statement, "While we were still weak, at the right time Christ died for the ungodly. . . . But God shows his love for us in that while we were yet sinners Christ died for us" (Rom. 5:6-8). Hope is that Christian grace which takes faith and love and reaches into tomorrow and all tomorrows.

Hope is so important in Christian belief that it may be used as a comprehensive term as is faith. Peter wrote, "Always be prepared to make a defense to any one who calls you to account for the hope that is in you" (1 Pet. 3:15). In this instance, hope stands for the entire Christian outlook, as faith so often does.

Faith and hope, however, are not the same. In several passages, of which 1 Corinthians 13 is the most popular, Paul made clear distinctions between faith, hope, and love. To blur the distinction is to invite distortion. John Knox stressed the difference in this way: "Love is God's love for us in Christ; faith is our receiving of this love; and hope is our laying hold upon, our confidence in, a future fulfillment."[1]

Christian hope is not optional. The Christian cannot be indifferent to the idea of resurrection and life after death. Biblical faith has a linear view of history. Along with the Hebrews, Christians believe that "in the beginning God created the heavens and the earth" (Gen. 1:1). This belief leads to the conviction that all of history moves toward an ultimate goal because God created with a purpose. Hope designates the human expectation that God will bring history to that meaningful conclusion.

The idea of creation is a theological belief. In Hebrews (11:3) we read, "By faith we understand that the world was created by the word of God." We confess a great deal of our faith when we say, "In the beginning God. . . ." We acknowledge that we believe that God is the Creator of all including us. Everything depends on God.

If God was in the beginning, then also we must see God at the end. John A. T. Robinson wrote "A Study of the Christian Doctrine of Last Things" under the title *In the End, God.*[2]

What Hope Is Not

Christian Hope Is Not Ghostly Survival

Survival beyond death is not a Christian idea, not even a religious idea. It appears to have been a belief of most ancient people. The burial customs, as unearthed by archaeologists, indicate that most people believed in some kind of survival after death. The Egyptian pharaohs made bountiful provisions for their existence beyond death which included a boat, food and clothing, and slave crews to ferry them across the sea to the land beyond death. Infant skeletons have been found in their earthenware coffins along with remains of dishes of food, toys, and trinkets. Biblical and nonbiblical writings attest to the almost universal belief in some kind of ghostly survival beyond the tomb.

In a remarkable book entitled *And the Life Everlasting*, John Baillie has documented the belief in ghostly survival among savage peoples, ancient Israelites, Greek philosophers, and thinkers from India and Persia. He concluded not only that such beliefs were almost universal but that usually they were not related to religion. Rather, they were "scientific" views, that is, they grew out of experience and observation.

While the almost universal belief in ghostly survival may give some general credibility to our specific Christian view of life beyond death, the ideas are radically different and should not be confused. The Christian view of life everlasting is related to belief in God and particularly to the resurrection of Jesus.

Christian Hope Is Not Nirvana

Sometimes people remark that nirvana is a parallel to the Christian belief in life after death. If one looks at the differences, the similarities are unimpressive. In Buddhist belief nirvana is the extinction of individual existence along with the extinction of all desire and passion. Nirvana is an escape from the endless transmigration of souls into an existence of unbearable repetition and boredom. While nirvana may be seen as escape from life into some kind of inactivity beyond desire, it is certainly no parallel for the Christian heaven. In Christian thought this life is the gift of God to be lived, not escaped. Heaven has continuity with earth; heaven is the completion of God's good creation which we already know on earth.

Christian Hope Is Not "Optimism" Nor "The Idea of Progress"

An optimistic view of human existence emerged in the liberal theology which began with Schleiermacher in the early nineteenth century and was particularly influential in the first third of the twentieth century. This "optimism" was grounded in the goodness of humanity. These thinkers believed in the perfectability of human life to be achieved by human effort. In fact, the "Idea of Progress" was a kind of historical parallel to the idea of biological evolution. Many of these thinkers believed that humanity was on an escalator going up—evolving as it were. The indefinite extension of this upward movement would, of course, result in some kind of utopia. The tragic wars and atrocities of the twentieth century destroyed such beliefs grounded in human goodness. Theologians returned to a serious view of human sin. This does not mean the abandonment of hope. It does mean, however, that Christian hope is grounded in God's work for and within us, not in our humanness. Christian hope is radically different from these ideas.

Christian Hope Is Not "Otherworldliness"

Periodically, extremists in Christian faith see the world as so evil that they try to live away from it. They live "in" the future. Occasionally they abandon their work, homes, and institutions and seek to live in an "otherworldly" way. Usually these persons have little, or no, regard for this world with its culture. They see this world as completely wicked. During a national assembly of a religious group inclined in this direction, the younger leaders sought to get their group to undertake projects of social improvement. Older leaders decried "trying to make this world a better place for people to go to hell from."

The negation of this world is an error growing out of a failure to distinguish between the world as God's creation and the world as human culture imposed on God's creation. Christian hope does, indeed, look to a future world, but that world is vitally related to this one.

Christian Hope Is Not Futurology

Modern technology which utilizes computers to store, sort, and relate vast bits of information has produced a new breed of people who predict the trends of the future. With some speculation beyond observable trends, these futurologists diagram the things which are likely to happen. While these projections may be of great help for business investments, they have no relationship whatsoever to the study before us. Christian hope is not interested in predicting the future. It certainly has no concern for projecting earthly trends. Rather, Christian eschatology deals with those themes related to God's actions of the past and present and the promises for His future.

Christian Hope Is Not Wishful Thinking

Christian beliefs have often been ridiculed as wishful thinking or the projection into the future or, to the ultimate, those ideas we know only partially now. The classic expression of this skepticism was formulated by Ludwig Feuerbach in a book entitled *The Essence of Christianity.* He maintained at great length and with much tedious illustration that all Christian beliefs are merely wishes. Heaven, of course, would be the ultimate wish for home.

If one grants Feuerbach his presuppositions, then, of course, there is no way to refute his conclusions. If, however, one begins with the biblical events recorded in Scripture and allows them to speak, the belief in eternal life is quite credible.

Christian Hope Is Not the Same as the Immortality of the Soul

We shall avoid misunderstanding later if we distinguish between the biblical view of humanity and that view which grew out of classical Greek philosophy. In biblical thought, human beings are always the creatures of God and are understood in terms of their creatureli-

ness. They are sinners capable of salvation, but dependent upon God
for that salvation. In the classical Greek view, men and women are
distinct because they have eternal souls residing temporarily in them.
This view is dualistic: a material body which is perishable and a soul
which automatically of itself lives forever (immortality). In this classical view from Greek antiquity, the soul is divine; it cannot die. Hence,
there was a minimizing of the importance of the body and this life,
and a maximizing of the divine soul. In gnosticism, the body came to
be regarded as evil of itself. Death was regarded as a blessing since
it released the soul to return to its original abode in the eternal realm.

Many Christian theologians worked Greek ideas of immortality
into Christian theology. Tertullian adopted the Stoic idea that the soul
was a substance separate from the body. Origen followed Plato in the
idea that the soul was preexistent, came to live in a human body,
survived the death of the body, and may come back to live in another
body. Augustine followed Plato's doctrine that the soul was naturally
immortal. Thomas Aquinas cast Christian theology in the philosophy
of Aristotle and argued for the natural immortality of the soul. In the
New Testament the language (Greek terms) in some passages appears
to teach this basic dichotomy of body and soul; but a word of caution
is in order.

In biblical faith, a human being is a unity (psychomatic) and can
be called both a living soul or a body. Biblical faith does not permit
the idea that the body as such is evil. Biblical faith looks upon us as
creatures of God entirely, and God's creation is good.[3]

In recent Protestant theology, the decided tendency has been to
abandon the idea of the immortality of the soul for several reasons.
(1) The Bible teaches that we, in our entirety, are creatures of God.
(2) The ideas of resurrection from the dead and the new creation are
the biblical ways of speaking of eternal life. (3) Only God is immortal
in the Bible. (4) Death is serious in biblical thought but is trivialized
in Platonic thought. (5) The Greek idea issues in a low estimate of the
human body, which biblical faith treats as the good creation of God.
(6) Greek thought sees the immortality of the soul as a natural endowment of human life and, as such, encourages pride; biblical faith sees

human life in its entirety dependent upon God. (7) The Christian belief in the resurrection from the dead and eternal life with God as a gift or new creation appears more in keeping with all of Christian theology.[4]

When we prefer to speak of the resurrection from the dead and eternal life as a new creation rather than a natural entitlement, we do not suggest any lessening of the hope for eternal life. We do, however, suggest that the belief in the resurrection as taught in Scripture is in every way superior to the pagan idea of "natural immortality"[5]

The notion that the human soul is divine would have been considered blasphemous in biblical thought. The idea of the immortality of the soul, however, does give indirect testimony to the universal, or almost universal, belief that there is life beyond death.

Approaches to the Study of Eschatology

During the preceding century, several different approaches have been taken to the study of eschatology. A brief survey may be helpful for our later study. Each approach claims to be based upon valid biblical interpretation.[6]

Consistent Eschatology

At the beginning of this century Albert Schweitzer, later known for his medical mission in Africa, published a pivotal book entitled *The Quest of the Historical Jesus.* Schweitzer recognized that most of the biographies of Jesus were sentimentalized versions of their author's wishes. He taught that the true Jesus was an apocalyptic teacher who saw Himself as the Son of man who would come on the clouds of heaven and bring the world to an eschatological end with the messianic kingdom.

Schweitzer believed that Jesus went to Jerusalem expecting this great event to happen. Instead, He was crucified. So, to Schweitzer, Jesus was a deluded hero. His view is called Consistent Eschatology because Schweitzer argued that the only way we can understand Jesus at all is through the consistent application of this eschatological view in our interpretation.

If Jesus was so mistaken, it is difficult to explain how the Christian faith emerged and flourished as it did.

Realized Eschatology

This view is usually identified with the scholar C. H. Dodd and his book entitled *The Parables of the Kingdom*. Dodd believed that the kingdom of God became a reality on this earth in the earthly ministry of Jesus. In other words, eschatology came to focus in the present kingdom and was not primarily concerned about the future.

The parables of Jesus teach about the kingdom. They have to do with human life here and now. The eschatological hope in the Old Testament came to fulfillment in the ministry of Jesus. In other words, all future eschatological hope has been realized in the present.

The view appears to neglect Jesus' teaching in those same parables which point to a future realization. No doubt a present aspect of the kingdom of God was realized in the ministry of Jesus. One must do a rather radical reinterpretation of much of the New Testament, however, to explain away the unrealized hope toward which we look in the future.

Inaugurated Eschatology

John A. T. Robinson advocated this view in his book *Jesus and His Coming*.[7] This view maintains the tension between the eschatological realization in the ministry of Jesus and the future hope. Jesus inaugurated the eschatological hope through His death and resurrection. In Jesus Christ the new age has dawned. The kingdom of God is at hand (Mark 1:15), has come (Luke 11:20), and is yet to come with suddenness.

This view is more in keeping with the New Testament teachings than the other views presented.

Eschatological Existence

Rudolf Bultmann, working out of an existentialist context, held a view similar to that of Schweitzer. Some interpreters simply refer to his view as Consistent Eschatology. There is a difference, however.

Bultmann believed that authentic human existence is the life of faith in God made known through Jesus Christ. With his existentialist approach, Bultmann saw all reality in the present moment. He disregarded the element of the future or considered it relatively unimportant. Authentic existence is the committed life of faith right now, in this moment. All of the eschatological statements of the New Testament come to fulfillment in this present moment. Authentic existence, then, is synonymous with eschatological existence. In other words, all of the New Testament statements about a future hope are demythologized into the present moment.[8]

Futurist Eschatology

Another school of thought interprets the eschatology of the New Testament strictly as a future event. Some adherents of this view expect a literal fulfillment of all Old Testament prophecies. They do not see the church as the fulfillment of many of them in the past. One example is Dispensational Eschatology.

Dispensational Eschatology has been based largely on the interpretative notes printed in the Scofield Reference Bible and popularized in such books as Hal Lindsay's *The Late Great Planet Earth.* Those who hold to these views believe theirs is the literal teaching of the Bible, and hence correct. Whereas many other interpreters see the church as a fulfillment of Israel, dispensationalists tend to guard a strict and permanent distinction between the two. The millennium of Revelation 20, though in a book of apocalyptic visions, is taken as literal history revealed and written in advance. They regard it as necessary to fulfill Old Testament promises which are applied literally to Israel (even the modern state of Israel). In their millennial kingdom, Christ will rule over a political kingdom on earth which includes unbelievers.

Dispensationalism, while claiming to be the true literal interpretation of the Bible, does not allow adequate consideration of the fact that the Bible includes literature in the form of poetry, allegory, parable, and apocalyptic. Dispensationalism tends to maintain a permanent distinction between Israel and the church in spite of the New

Testament teaching that the church is the new people of God and
Israel has been fulfilled in the church (Matt. 21:43; 1 Pet. 2:9-10). This
view would place Christ on a throne of an earthly kingdom governing
by force which is exactly what He refused to do in His earthly life.

Theologies of Hope

In the wake of World War II, theologians have emerged champion-
ing the theme of hope. Examples are Jürgen Moltmann and Wolfhart
Pannenberg. In a sense their theology is not an eschatology in the
customary use of the term. Rather, they interpret the whole body of
theology in terms of the future. Pannenberg, for instance, would see
the future as the measure of reality rather than past history. Most of
us are inclined to think of history as real and of the future as something which does not have reality yet. Pannenberg, however, thinks
that all reality is really future. What we call history is not complete
yet, so it is not completely real. Only the future, then, is really real

Pannenberg started with Jesus' announcement that the kingdom of
heaven is at hand—just over the horizon. God calls us to live in and
for the future. The resurrection of Jesus Christ from the dead was the
classical future event which broke into the present to give us this
vision of the future—reality.[9]

The Theologies of Hope have provided an encouragement in a time
of pessimism. They have stressed again the creative power of human
hope. They have not, however, replaced the study of Christian hope
as the end of salvation.

The Approach in This Study

I do not know of a title which I would apply to the approach of
this volume. Numerous factors are included. Let me state my presuppositions which will be the guidelines.

Jesus Christ Is the Foundation

God has chosen to reveal Himself in the historical events recorded
in the Bible. The classic example in the Old Testament is the deliverance from Egypt, the Exodus. The central event of all revelation is

Jesus Christ. All Christian theology must stand on the foundation of Christ and be judged by Him or forfeit the name *Christian.* Any doctrine that is taught by or grounded in Jesus Christ deserves consideration. Any doctrine that is not so based is questionable. Any doctrine that is not compatible with the revelation of God in Christ must be disregarded.

The Bible Is the Textbook

The primary source of all information to be used in formulating Christian doctrines is the canonical Scripture. These writings stand in a direct relationship with apostles, or eyewitnesses. They are faithful in their portrait of Jesus. They are inspired and authoritative not only in their authorship but also when they are read today under the guidance of the Holy Spirit.

Jesus Taught Us to Live in Hope

Jesus began His preaching on the kingdom of God. He promised to come again. He rose from the dead and appeared. The eschatological hope is a vital part of Jesus' message.

Christian Hope Is the Purpose of God

The purpose of God in creation and redemption issues in those themes of hope planted in human hearts by Jesus Christ. Eternal life is not something to which we aspire and gain; rather, it is the purpose of God toward which He moves His creatures.

Christian Hope Is a Human Response to God

God has taken the initiative in revealing Himself to us. We respond to God by believing, loving, and hoping. Faith, hope, and love are human graces born in response to God's marvelous grace. Then, the expectations of Christian hope are not ambitious wishes or selfish desires. They are the genuine human responses to the great gifts of God to us. Hope is a response to God, just as faith is. To regard it so will remove every hint of selfishness from it and spare us the pride born of works.

Hope as Response to God

What I call "Hope as Response to God" is close to what Val J. Sauer[10] called "Systematic Eschatology." He cited the systematic theological approach which identifies several "systematic" themes which appear in Scripture and in a sequence: death, Christ's return, resurrection, intermediate state, final judgment, and final states. These themes are present in many passages, and are generally recognized as major views.

In this approach to Christian hope, I see these major themes evoking a response from us toward God. The present response of faith issues in hope. The hope is genuinely present as a powerful element in life even though its full realization will be in the future.

Following this approach, I will not give much attention to purgatory because it is not taught in Scripture. I will not give a major role to millennialism. The theme appears only in one chapter in the Bible in the figurative language of an apocalypse. On the other hand, I will give very serious consideration to the kingdom of God to which belief the millennium bears an important witness.

We shall try to see what the Bible teaches, review what other Christians have understood the Bible to teach, state the beliefs, and give reasons for holding these to be true.

Notes

1. John Knox, *Christ and the Hope of Glory* (New York and Nashville: Abingdon Press, 1960), p. 25.

2. John A. T. Robinson, *In the End, God* (London: James Clark & Co., LTD, 1950).

3. For a detailed study of the Greek idea of soul, see Dale Moody, *The Word of Truth* (Grand Rapids: William B. Eerdmans Publishing Company, 1981), pp. 170-181.

4. For a study of death and immortality see Otto Weber, *Foundations of Dogmatics*, Darrell L. Guder, trans. (Grand Rapids: William B. Eerdmans Publishing Company, 1983), 2:667 *ff.*

5. George Eldon Ladd, *The Last Things, an Eschatology for Laymen* (Grand Rapids: William B. Eerdmans Publishing Company, 1978), p. 31.

6. For a discussion of these various approaches, see Chapter 2 of Val J. Sauer, *The Eschatology Handbook* (Atlanta: John Knox Press, 1981).

7. John A. T. Robinson, *Jesus and His Coming* (New York and Nashville: Abingdon Press, 1957). See also Sauer.

8. For a summary of Bultmann's views and a bibliography of his writings, see Morris Ashcraft, "Life in Faith—Authentic Existence," *Rudolf Bultmann* (Waco: Word Books, Publisher, 1972).

9. Jürgen Moltmann, *Theology of Hope* (New York and Evanston: Harper & Row, Publishers, 1967); Ewert H. Cousins, ed., *Hope and the Future of Man* (Philadelphia: Fortress Press, 1972); for a bibliography and study of Pannenberg, see E. Frank Tupper, *The Theology of Wolfhart Pannenberg* (Philadelphia: The Westminster Press, 1973).

10. Sauer, pp. 28 *ff.*

2
Why Hope?

> But the angel said to the women, "Do not be afraid; for I know that you seek Jesus who was crucified. He is not here; for he has risen, as he said. Come, see the place where he lay" (Matt. 28:5-6).
>
> Jesus said to her, "I am the resurrection and the life; he who believes in me, though he die, yet shall he live, and whoever lives and believes in me shall never die" (John 11:25-26).

In the previous chapter I stated the reasons for discussing Christian expectations under the heading of hope rather than eschatology. Now, before looking at the specific beliefs growing out of that hope, let us consider why we think our beliefs about the future are justified.

Why do we have hope? Why does Christian hope endure? Do we have adequate reasons to justify our hope? Can we give a convincing case for the hope that is in us? I wish to propose four reasons for our hope, or a four-part answer to the question, Why hope?

Our Christian hope stands on the following foundation: (1) the resurrection of Jesus; (2) hope is central in the gospel; (3) the Old Testament teachings point toward Christian hope; and (4) hope is more reasonable than the alternatives.

The Resurrection of Jesus

The Christian belief in a future resurrection is grounded in the resurrection of Jesus. This, alone, is an adequate foundation for our belief in our future resurrection. The early Christians were certain that Jesus, who had been killed, had been raised from the dead. They declared that He had appeared on several occasions to individuals, to small and large groups of people. The fact of His resurrection is argued on the basis of the following witnesses.

The Witnesses of the Resurrection

The empty tomb.—Thousands watched Jesus' crucifixion. The disciples were there. When the soldiers came to break the legs of the three crucified men, they found that Jesus was already dead (John 19:33). All of the Gospels witness to the fact that Jesus was dead (Matt. 27:50; Mark 15:37; Luke 23:46). The Book of Acts repeatedly referred to His death using such words as "slain" (2:23, KJV), "killed" (3:15), and "crucified" (2:36). Jesus' killers were murderers (7:52).

The witnesses reported that the guarded tomb was empty on that first Easter morning. The details vary somewhat, as one would expect, but the witness is uniform—there was no corpse in the tomb. Angelic messengers told the visitors to the tomb that Jesus had been raised (Matt. 28:7; Mark 16:6; Luke 24:7).

If there were no other witnesses, the empty tomb would hardly be conclusive. There are, however, other witnesses.

The postresurrection witnesses.—John reported that Mary Magdalene was the first witness to see the resurrected Jesus (20:1,11). Matthew reported that Jesus appeared to the eleven remaining disciples in Galilee (Matt. 28:16). Luke reported (24:13-35) that Jesus appeared to two persons on the way to the village of Emmaus and later ate broiled fish (v. 42). The longer ending of Mark includes the detail that Mary Magdalene had first seen the risen Lord (Mark 16:9).

Paul, in 1 Corinthians, which was written about AD 55-57, gave a report of the resurrection appearances which is earlier than our written Gospels. He listed appearances to Cephas, then to the twelve disciples, then to a crowd of more than five hundred, then to James, then to all of the apostles and finally to Paul (1 Cor. 15:6-8).[1]

In terms of historical witnesses, we have more evidence for the resurrection of Jesus than we do for most events in ancient history. No one would ever think of doubting the "happenedness" of other events reported in history with such an array of witnesses. First

Corinthians was written less than thirty years after the crucifixion of Jesus. Numerous witnesses would have still been alive. A false report would have been refuted.

The witness of the living church.—Apart from those remaining eyewitnesses, the early Christians would be only secondary witnesses, but their testimony speaks to the credibility of Jesus' resurrection. Galatians, probably written in AD 49, is one of the earliest Christian writings which we possess. For almost two decades after the events, the early church lived on the oral witness about Jesus. These persons risked their lives and eternity on their belief that Jesus had been raised.

Throughout the centuries, the church has borne its witness to the power of the resurrection rather convincingly.

Questions About the Resurrection

Arguments and questions.—The witnesses gave variations in the details. For instance, the two disciples on the way to Emmaus did not recognize Jesus at first. Cleopas, one of them, indicated that the women had gone to the tomb, learned that Jesus' body was not there, and reported seeing angels who said He was alive (Luke 24: 13-31). There is some uncertainty about how many times Jesus appeared. One of the twelve even refused to believe the report at first.

By the time of Matthew's Gospel, a denial of the resurrection was circulating which spoke of a bribe paid to the soldiers to say that the disciples had stolen the body of Jesus while the guards were asleep (Matt. 28:11-15). Some have denied Jesus' resurrection by saying that He was not really dead, merely in a coma or swoon. Others have tried to reduce all resurrection appearances to apparitions or visions. There are numerous summaries of these denials.[2]

Rudolf Bultmann, in more recent times, doubted the historical reliability of the Gospels, thinking the historical fact unimportant. He taught that the Easter faith meant only that Jesus was alive and with the disciples. Bultmann was not concerned with the historical witnesses. He was concerned with Christ's spiritual presence. In other words, the resurrection was not an historical event like the crucifixion; rather, it was a matter of faith.[3]

The early Christian witnesses insisted, however, that Jesus who had been crucified had, indeed, been raised from the dead. If one begins with a presuppostion that a dead person cannot be raised to life again, then, of course, one will seek another way to interpret Jesus' resurrection. Interpreters have often dealt with Jesus' resurrection on the basis of this presupposition. While we cannot explain the mystery surrounding His resurrection, we are convinced, as were the early Christians, that His resurrection was real. They spoke of a bodily resurrection.

The resurrection of the body.—In the Western world, conditioned by Greek thought, we continue to think of body and soul as a basic dichotomy, as if each somehow exists in independence of the other. Biblical faith, on the other hand, speaks of human existence as a unity including both spiritual and physical characteristics. In the biblical tradition, one could hardly conceive of a human being as merely a body (without the spiritual nature) or as a mere soul (without a bodily existence).

The New Testament witnesses wrote of the risen Lord as the same Jesus who had been crucified. Mystery remained, however. Whatever kind of body Jesus was we cannot say with certainty. They spoke of a "bodily" resurrection, designating a real event and about the same person Jesus. Paul struggled with the question about what kind of bodies we will be in the resurrection. He stated that we have, or are, spiritual bodies. Evidently, he meant that a transformation takes place. The resurrection does not mean merely a literal raising of the physical flesh; we are spiritual bodies. We are bodies, however. For this reason, Christians have always favored a confessional statement including bodily resurrection (1 Cor. 15:44).

Following a strict definition of the word *historical,* Hans Küng said that the resurrection of Jesus was not historical, but was a "real event."[4] He meant that disinterested bystanders would not have seen the risen Lord. Jesus was known only by believers after the resurrection, but God really raised Jesus. The resurrection was real. Distinctions of this kind are rather confusing to most persons. This view sounds like Jesus was a spiritual presence only, which was Bultmann's view.

The New Testament speaks of other raisings from the dead. Jesus raised the son of a widow in the village of Nain (Luke 7:11-17). Jesus restored the dead daughter of Jairus to life (Luke 8:40-42, 49-56). John reported that Jesus restored Lazarus to life after he had been dead for four days (John 11:1-44).

These raisings were not resurrections. The persons named were restored to life but died again. Jesus was raised to a different kind of, or transformed, life never to die again. Our hope for the resurrection from the dead is a hope for eternal life, not the mere resuscitation of corpses.

Resurrection-Hope Is Central in the Gospel

The earliest Christians were Hebrews. They believed in God as He had made Himself known in Israel's history. The Old Testament was their Bible. Jesus Christ, though continuous with the Old Covenant, brought something radically new. It is called Christian faith. It is different from Hebrew faith in the sense that it is a fulfillment. The Christian message, or Word of God, goes beyond the Old Testament. What is this message, this gospel?

The Christian Message

In the earliest Christian preaching.—About seven weeks after the death of Jesus, Peter preached in the Temple area at Pentecost. Peter stressed these themes: Jesus of Nazareth was a man whom God attested by His wonders and mighty works; Jesus was delivered up and crucified by lawless men; God raised Jesus from the dead; Peter and the others were witnesses of these events; God had made Jesus both Lord and Christ; in the name of Jesus people may have the forgiveness of their sins (Acts 2:22-29). The raising of Jesus was a vital element in that message.

In the early summaries of Christian faith.—Paul gave an early summary of the major themes of Christian beliefs (1 Cor. 15:3-8).

They are: (1) "I delivered to you as of first importance what I also received." Paul had not invented the gospel but had received it from the witnesses. (2) "Christ died for our sins in accordance with the scriptures." (3) "He was raised on the third day in accordance with the scriptures." (4) "He appeared to Cephas . . . to the twelve . . . to more than five hundred at one time . . . to James . . . to all the apostles . . . to me."

Peter gave an early summary of Christian beliefs (1 Pet. 1:3-9). These themes are: (1) God is the Father of our Lord Jesus Christ. (2) Through Christ we are born anew. (3) Faith is a living hope. (4) Faith was brought through the resurrection of Jesus Christ from the dead. (5) We have an inheritance in heaven. (6) God keeps us safe. (7) God continues to relate to us in our joys and sufferings, thereby preparing us for ultimate salvation.

In both summaries, the resurrection of Jesus is central in the faith, and points on to our belief in the future.

Major themes of the apostles' preaching.—In 1936 a well-known New Testament scholar, C. H. Dodd, published a small but important volume entitled *The Apostolic Preaching and Its Development.*[5] Having studied carefully the preaching and teaching in the New Testament's earliest sections, he summarized the themes: (1) the new age had dawned in the coming of Christ; (2) Christ came from the family lineage of David; (3) Christ died to deliver us; (4) He was buried; (5) He rose on the third day according to the Scriptures; (6) He was exalted to the right hand of God; (7) He will come again, and; (8) forgiveness of sin and the Holy Spirit come to those who believe in Christ.

Perhaps I have made the mistake against which I have warned the readers. Perhaps I have stressed the resurrection of Jesus to the point of neglecting the other themes. Note, however, in every instance the resurrection of Jesus is an indispensable element in the message and points on to a future hope for us who believe in Him.

The Meaning of His Resurrection

Christ's life, teachings, death, and resurrection form the basis of Christian belief. Belief is more than holding to doctrines. It is personal trust in, or commitment to, God as revealed in Christ. Belief is more than believing "that" Christ died and rose again for us. Faith is believing "in" Christ. This comes about within us through hearing the gospel (Rom. 1:17). We think about it, become convinced that it is true, and then we trust Jesus.

Christ's resurrection from the dead stands in a vital relationship to His life and death and to our faith. His resurrection is that event which removes our hesitation and beckons our response. Dale Moody correctly commented, "All stands or falls on this event."[6]

I once heard people arguing that our faith in Christ would not be affected one way or the other if Jesus' corpse had remained in the grave. They speculated that if the archaeologists had found His grave, identified it and the skeleton with certainty, and established beyond doubt that He had not been raised, it would really make no difference to us. I think if that had happened our faith would have received a devastating blow. Bruce Vawter maintained that our faith was precisely the belief that God had raised Jesus from the dead in a special act.[7]

Confirmation of God's presence.—At Caesarea Philippi Peter had recognized God's revelation in Christ as the Messiah. The disciples pledged Him their lives. Jesus' crucifixion left them alone. His resurrection confirmed God's presence. On one occasion while Christ was with them, He asked the disciples if they also would go away. Peter responded, "Lord, to whom shall we go? You have the words of eternal life: and we have believed, and have come to know, that you are the Holy One of God" (John 6:68-69).

The resurrection confirms that we will never be alone again. In doubt we feel abandoned. We wonder if God is really there. Are we alone? All alone? Is the black boundary of death all there is? The resurrection of Jesus says that God is with us now and will be with us beyond death.

Affirmation of God's promises.—Biblical faith is based on the promises of God. These promises inspire hope and endow life with meaning and destiny. The resurrection of Jesus is the boldest declaration that God keeps His promises.

Jesus predicted His own death and resurrection (Mark 8:31-32; 9:31-32; 10:33-34). The disciples didn't understand then. After the resurrection, they did. God kept the promise. When you and I doubt, we need to read the New Testament accounts of Jesus' resurrection from the dead.

Reminder of providence.—The biblical writers repeatedly remind us that God who created the world continues to guide and sustain His creation toward its goal and His purpose. The saga of Joseph in Genesis illustrates this watchcare. Paul declared it clearly in Romans 8:28, "We know that in everything God works for good with those who love him, who are called according to his purpose."

Peter saw the providence of God in the crucifixion. He condemned those who crucified Jesus, but interpreted, "this Jesus, delivered up according to the definite plan and foreknowledge of God, you crucified and killed by the hands of lawless men. But God raised him up" (Acts 2:23-24).

The resurrection of Jesus speaks to us that we can be assured of the providence of God in our lives and destinies.

Old Testament Antecedents of Christian Hope

It is a serious mistake for Christians to read their Christian beliefs back into the Old Testament. It is equally serious to ignore the teachings of the Old Testament which so often shed light on Christian themes. Some eschatological themes are quite clear in the Old Testament and are helpful in Christian understanding.

Examples Related to Present Life

Covenant faith and promise.—The Hebrews believed that God had called them into a special relationship with Him, a covenant relationship. Abraham and his descendants were pilgrims on a journey undergirded by the promise of God. Although the goal of that journey may have been a Promised Land in Canaan, it was a promise which spoke of hope and destiny.

Covenant and promise saturate the life of the Hebrews. The most beautiful statement of it, whether limited to this world or including the next, is the oft-repeated "I will be your God, and you shall be my people" (Jer. 7:23).

The purpose of Israel understood as a covenant with God leads to a pilgrimage based on promise. This kind of faith inevitably leads to eschatolgical beliefs.

Judgment on the nation.—The covenant with Israel raised the question of God's expectation and Israel's faithfulness. God could not forget Israel. He guided the nation, correcting her when she sinned. The prophets clearly proclaimed this correction, or judgment, as the Day of the Lord.

Amos is a good example of this understanding of judgment. He proclaimed the coming Day of the Lord as a time of vindication or condemnation (Amos 5:18-20). He employed the parable of a plumb line suspended by the wall of the building. When God came to judge Israel, He would vindicate the righteousness which the judgment revealed; He would condemn the injustice revealed in the judgment (7:7-9).

Judgment on the whole world.—The Old Testament story so features Israel that we could overlook God's concern for and involvement in the other nations. God is Lord of all. All nations come under God's judgment. Several Old Testament writers dealt with this theme. Isaiah is a good example. He spoke of all nations coming under God's judgment, hence they are included in God's purpose (Isa. 2:2 *ff.*).

Judgment on individuals.—In the previous illustrations God's judgment was general. Jeremiah and Ezekiel reflect a notable emphasis, or change, from the nation to the individual. Both of them quoted the old adage, "The fathers have eaten sour grapes, and the children's teeth are set on edge." Then, both went on to stress that individuals can no longer deny their individual responsibility by hiding in the family, nation, race, or inheritance. Rather, every person is responsible for his or her own sin (Jer. 31:29; Ezek. 18:2). This dramatic announcement became the foundation for the later development of eschatology related to individuals.

Beliefs About Life Beyond Death

The New Testament concept of heaven is not found in the Old Testament. Scholars recognize that early Israel shared with most ancient peoples the belief in continued existence beyond death in a shadowy netherworld. They also recognize that Israel's faith included the idea of a general resurrection and judgment before the end of the Old Testament.[8]

Sheol.—The Hebrews believed that a kind of existence continued after death in a region outside the earth but accessible to God. Sheol was not a desirable place. Its inhabitants did not have the freedom of return (Job 16:22), although they might have been called up by the living for consultation (1 Sam. 28:13).[9]

Even the shadow of Sheol is occasionally penetrated by the light of hope. The psalmist wrote, "For thou dost not give me up to Sheol, or let thy godly one see the Pit" (Ps. 16:10). Again, "But God will ransom my soul from the power of Sheol, for he will receive me" (49:15). Also, "Thou dost guide me with thy counsel, and afterward thou wilt receive me to glory" (73:24). These expressions of hope are not the same as the New Testament hope for resurrection, but they are hopeful.

Job's question.—Job apparently held to the popular notion of Sheol; but in the depth of suffering, Job's hope resisted despair. His faith in God voiced a question which camouflaged a hope. "Oh that thou wouldest hide me in Sheol, that thou wouldest conceal me until thy wrath be past, that thou wouldest appoint me a set time, and remember me! If a man die, shall he live again?" (14:13-14).

The question was like a groan of agony by a man on the brink of despair. It was a question, however, which concealed a dawning hope, "If a man die, shall he live again?" Job did not receive or state a clear answer. He even went deeper into pessimism. His question, however, indirectly confessed a faith in God who loves us so much that He must have more in store for us than this life.

A resurrection in Daniel.—The only certain statement in the Old Testament about a general resurrection is in Daniel. "Many of those who sleep in the dust of the earth shall awake, some to everlasting life, and some to shame and everlasting contempt" (12:2). In Isaiah there is a statement, "Thy dead shall live, their bodies shall rise" (26:19), that may be the earliest biblical statement about a resurrection. Some would interpret this as they do the dry bones of Ezekiel's prophecy.

By the time of Daniel, the idea of a general resurrection appears to have been common. In the New Testament era we find that the Pharisees believed in a resurrection from the dead, but the Sadducees did not.

The Reasonableness of Hope

Ludwig Feuerbach launched the most serious attack ever made on religion in general and Christianity in particular. In *The Essence Of Christianity,* he maintained that every Christian belief is merely a wish, a projection of some finite wish into the infinite.[10] Feuerbach did not distinguish between wish and hope. There is a difference. Hope is grounded in theological beliefs. It is not mere wishing. It rests upon the solid foundation of historical revelation in Jesus Christ.

Hope Inevitably Grows Out of Belief in God

Believing in God leads to and requires hope in the future. All of the reasons for believing in God, therefore, support the belief that God will complete His creation and bring it to His purposive culmination. The difference between wishing and hoping is belief in God. Human beings wish out of their self-centeredness. When their lives are centered on God by faith, they can hope for God's future acts.

Human Experience Calls for Hope

The temporary nature of life, the uncertainty of existence, along with a sense of purpose cry out for hope. Indeed, we "plow in hope" and we "thresh in hope" (1 Cor. 9:10). In hope we bear and bring up our children, earn our daily bread, and retire to rest. In hope we make the lonely journey to the graveside with loved ones. One day we shall go there ourselves—in hope. If life has any meaning at all, our hope makes sense.

The Universal Expressions of Hope Are Arguments for It

The idea of Sheol, or ghostly survival, speaks a convincing word that this life is not all there is. Even negative nirvana gives an indirect witness to the universal longing which reaches beyond death. Toys and trinkets in the ancient burial jars of infants speak a persuasive word for hope beyond death.

The Unfinished Nature of Life Speaks of Hope

All of our lives bear a label which reads *unfinished.* This is especially true of those who for any reason die prematurely. It is also true for those who live long lives. Each of us, at best, is like a piece of unfinished furniture. We need more sanding, rubbing, and finishing. What has been accomplished is obviously worthy and reveals an intent well underway. To deny completion is contradictory to the idea of purpose.

Meaning in Life Calls for Future Hope

Unless our lives are a cruel joke, there must be a life beyond death. We live with purpose and meaning. The disappointments of history and individual life, however, cry out for another chance on the other side. Our collective existence in the world is often marred and distorted, but even the distortions conceal a struggle for meaning, an expression of purpose. Even when our human aspirations lead us to excess, cruelty, or mistreatment of others, they speak of something in human existence which needs more time or another chance.

Hope adds an element of meaning and purpose to life. Human lives are lifted by this hope. Surely the creative power of hope must be an expression of the creative power of God in His universe. Hope is also "patient and kind." Hope is "not jealous or boastful" either. Hope is "not arrogant or rude." Hope lives with love.

Hope Is More Reasonable Than the Alternatives

We cannot prove to the skeptic that our faith in God is real. Nor can we prove that our hope for life beyond death is true. We have, however, a very persuasive witness about the resurrection of Jesus and God's promise to us. Human life abounds with a sense of meaning which points beyond this life.

The opposite of hope is despair, or meaninglessness. Hope is by far the better choice. Even if there were no life after death, living in hope is preferable to meaninglessness.

Between hope and despair (or meaninglessness) there are other possible alternatives. Agnosticism is not much better than meaninglessness. Indifference is beneath the dignity of a human being. Doubt, or openness to the possibility, can be a much preferable alternative than denial or despair.

Believing in the Christian hope of life eternal makes more sense than settling for any other choice. So, let us look more specifically at the content of Christian hope.

Notes

1. See any harmony of the Gospels, Gospel parallels, or a Bible dictionary on the "Resurrection" for a summary and comparison of resurrection appearances.

2. Ray Summers, *The Life Beyond* (Nashville: Broadman Press, 1959), pp. 34 *ff.*

3. For summary and sources in Bultmann, see Morris Ashcraft, "Makers of the Modern Theological Mind," *Rudolf Bultmann* (Waco: Word Books, Publisher, 1972), p. 70.

4. Hans Küng, *Eternal Life?* Edward Quinn, trans. (Garden City: Doubleday & Company, 1984), p. 105.

5. C. H. Dodd, *The Apostolic Preaching and Its Development* (London: Hodder & Stoughton Limited, 1936), p. 17.

6. Dale Moody, *The Hope of Glory* (Grand Rapids: William B. Eerdmans Publishing Company, 1964), p. 83.

7. Bruce Vawter, *This Man Jesus* (Garden City: Doubleday & Company, Inc., 1973), p. 45.

8. R. H. Charles, *A Critical History of the Doctrine of a Future Life in Israel, in Judaism and in Christianity* (London: Adam and Charles Black, 1913).

9. See T. H. Gaster, "Dead, Abode of the," *Interpreter's Dictionary of the Bible* (New York and Nashville: Abingdon Press, 1962), 1:787-788.

10. Ludwig Feuerbach, *The Essence of Christianity,* George Eliot, trans. (New York: Harper & Brothers Publishers, 1957).

3
Hope and Death

And the soldiers led him away inside the palace (that is, the praetorium); and they called together the whole battalion. And they clothed him in a purple cloak, and plaiting a crown of thorns they put it on him. And they began to salute him, "Hail, King of the Jews!" And they struck his head with a reed, and spat upon him, and they knelt down in homage to him. And when they had mocked him, they stripped him of the purple cloak, and put his own clothes on him. And they led him out to crucify him. And when the sixth hour had come, there was darkness over the whole land until the ninth hour. And at the ninth hour Jesus cried with a loud voice, "Eloi, Eloi, lama sabachthani?" which means, "My God, my God, why hast thou forsaken me?" And some of the bystanders hearing it said, "Behold, he is calling Elijah." And one ran and, filling a sponge full of vinegar, put it on a reed and gave it to him to drink, saying, "Wait, let us see whether Elijah will come to take him down." And Jesus uttered a loud cry, and breathed his last (Mark 15:16-20,33-37).

Death invades our lives by claiming those dearest to us. Death also stalks our own lives as an enemy standing in the shadows waiting, watching. Death is always an intruder, never a welcomed guest.

During the final preparation of this manuscript, death took two of those very dear to me. Dr. John Ed Steely died suddenly of a heart attack on Good Friday. We had been college freshmen together, seminary students together, friends of a lifetime, and colleagues on a seminary faculty. While he was ready to go, I was not ready to go on without him. One month ago my sister, Eunice Balfour, lost her

40

struggle against lung cancer. Although we had known for about a year that death was coming, we were not ready for it when it came.

Paul encouraged us, as he did the Thessalonians, when he wrote, "But we would not have you ignorant, brethren, concerning those who are asleep, that you may not grieve as others do who have no hope" (1 Thess. 4:13). Indeed, we have hope. To be sure, we do not grieve as those who have no hope. We do grieve, however, because death remains a part of the dark reality of human existence.

A definition of death does not come easy. The physicians and the coroners say when a person is dead by determining the failure of the different vital functions of the body. When we speak of death, we certainly include biological or clinical death. We could define human death as a purely natural event, like the death of animals. Emil Brunner was certainly correct, however, when he said, "But the truth is that man does not die like other higher animals, any more than he lives like them."[1] Human death, like life, has mystery about it.

The term, and idea, *death,* appears in the Bible in a variety of ways. It certainly refers to biological death in most cases. On other occasions, it can refer to a kind of separation from life even for one who is still biologically alive. The term also designates the spiritual reality quite apart from physical death. The term "second death" was even used in the Book of Revelation to designate the eternal separation from God which befalls the wicked after the final judgment.

If we are to understand the meaning of death in the Bible, we shall have to be willing to make distinctions which take into account the spiritual dimensions, as well as the physical. Some theologians like to distinguish three types of death: (1) spiritual, (2) physical, and (3) eternal.[2]

Death as the Normal End of Life

In the early period of Old Testament history, people did not have a view of eternal life such as we have now based on the resurrection of Jesus Christ. They seemed to believe that the shades of persons continued to exist in some shadowy netherworld, but it was a gloomy existence. In the face of this, numerous Scripture passages indicate that the people accepted death as the normal end of life. When Joshua gave his charge to Israel as his own death approached, he said, "Now I am about to go the way of all the earth" (Josh. 23:14).

One can find numerous statements about death in the Old Testament, but we shall look at only three illustrations which seem to be representative.

Death in Ripe Old Age

While Abram was sleeping the Lord told him about the destiny of the Hebrew people. Then the Lord said, "As for yourself, you shall go to your fathers in peace; you shall be buried in a good old age" (Gen. 15:15). A similar statement was made about Isaac: "And Isaac breathed his last; and he died and was gathered to his people, old and full of days, and his sons Esau and Jacob buried him" (35:29).

The inevitability and the acceptance of death as the normal end of life is also indicated by the Hebrew understanding of what was a normal life span. In the early Old Testament this was regarded as 120 years. "Then the Lord said, 'My spirit shall not abide in man for ever, for he is flesh, but his days shall be one hundred and twenty years' " (Gen. 6:3). In the later period of the Old Testament, the normal life span was understood to be seventy years. The psalmist wrote, "The years of our life are threescore and ten, or even by reason of strength fourscore; yet their span is but toil and trouble; they are soon gone, and we fly away" (90:10).

Death as Being Gathered to One's People

We noted in the passages cited from Genesis that death was like being gathered to one's people. The conclusion of the good life was to be buried in the family cemetery with one's fathers.

One common way of speaking of death in the Old Testament was to say that a person slept with his fathers. It was said that "David slept with his fathers" (1 Kings 2:10) and also of Solomon, "And Solomon slept with his fathers, and was buried in the city of David his father; and Rehoboam his son reigned in his stead" (1 Kings 11:43).

When Death Is Tragic

In the Old Testament, a person's life could be regarded as a good life if that person attained the normal life span, left children who would perpetuate the name and family, and was buried with honor in the cemetery with his or her parents.

It was tragic, however, if one of these elements was missing. If one died prematurely, it was a tragedy. When Hezekiah had recovered from an illness he had thought to be terminal, he reminisced, "I said, In the noontide of my days I must depart; I am consigned to the gates of Sheol for the rest of my years. I said, I shall not see the Lord in the land of the living; I shall look upon man no more among the inhabitants of the world" (Isa. 38:10-11). This lamentation portrays the tragedy of death in the prime of life. It also indicates the belief that life had been cut off because Hezekiah indicated he would spend the rest of his years in Sheol. The statement clearly indicates that the arena in which we live and are related to God and other people is in this life. Sheol advertises neither joy nor promise.

The Hebrews developed and practiced a careful procedure for the burial of the dead partly because of the respect for the human life and body and partly because the family grave was a tangible reminder of history. They had meticulous laws and customs about touching the dead. They did not like for corpses to be exposed or mutilated.

Death as the Enemy

Throughout the teachings of Scripture, death appears as the enemy of every person. Death is a threat to the very existence of a person. For one who is living, the thought of not being at all is horrible. It is an even more devastating thought to consider those whom we love and to be faced with their not being any more.

The Seriousness of Death

As a minister, I have often been with the families of those recently deceased. I have heard other Christians, and sometimes ministers, make such statements as, "He is better off than we are," or "God wants this person to be with Him," or "It is God's will and who are we to question God?"

We trivialize death and give no honor to God when we speak so flippantly. Certainly the bereaved should be encouraged with appropriate biblical promises of resurrection and life beyond. Comfort should be offered the grieving. Yet somehow I feel that, in our haste to comfort, we treat death as if it were less serious than it is.

There are occasions on which a person has lived victoriously to a ripe old age and has been left not only alone but also worn-out and ill. If these people are suffering a great deal and have no prospect of getting well, we may reason in our more practical moments that death is the better way. There is still a tragic loss when a human being dies. Death leaves a vacancy which no one can ever fill. Death is serious to the one who faces it.

We could cite heroic souls who risked and lost their own lives for others. We can award medals posthumously to those heroes. Even if we do not care, however, a circle of loved ones, family, and friends do care and grieve not only now but will also miss them for decades. Death is a robber.

Several decades ago the Scottish theologian John Baillie wrote a little book entitled *And the Life Everlasting.* In that book he discussed those people who say that they are not interested in life after death, that they are concerned only about this world. Professor Baillie suggested that a person making that statement and seeing his own beloved die and believing that death is permanent would not say, "I don't care about life after death." Baillie reasoned that such a person would be a traitor to his beloved and to all of the love they had shared. He affirmed, "He has no right not to care," and "He has no right not to be sad."[3]

Even if I reach the stage that I do not care about my own death, I should be very cautious about applying that same lack of concern to anyone else.

The Universality of Death

It is so obvious that we all die that a brief mention of this fact will suffice. The question about death figured in the first temptation experience of the parents of the race. Adam and Eve were tempted to trespass on God's domain and deny their own limited existence. The tempter said, "You will not die" (Gen. 3:4). Adam and Eve sought to deny or escape the creaturely boundary of death. We human beings are creatures and, as such, are limited in both time and space. Our human lives will come to an end. We, too, shall die.

Paul understood the fact of the universality of death to be as inevitable as our common humanity. He wrote, "For as in Adam all die, so also in Christ shall all be made alive" (1 Cor. 15:22). Paul argued the universality of sin (Rom. 3:23) and that "the wages of sin is death" (6:23).

Even the Son of God who came to earth in human form died. The New Testament and the statements of faith based upon it are correct in their insistence that Jesus was really dead. Only through death could He completely identify Himself with the human beings whom He came to save.

The Reign of Death

When Paul was teaching how Christ died for us in order to save us, he reasoned, "Therefore as sin came into the world through one man and death through sin, and so death spread to all men because all men sinned. . . . Yet death reigned from Adam to Moses, even over those whose sins were not like the transgression of Adam, who was a type of the one who was to come" (Rom. 5:12-14). The expression "death reigned" could possibly mean only that death prevailed or that death continued.

There is a suggestion, however, that death is regarded in an almost personal way. Death and Sheol were personified in places in the Old Testament. In Proverbs death was a kind of monster which swallowed people. Proverbs 1:12 reads, "like Sheol let us swallow them alive and whole, like those who go down to the Pit." Isaiah said, "Sheol has enlarged its appetite and opened its mouth beyond measure" (Isa. 5:14). This personification, or near personification, of death is also repeated in the New Testament.

Paul almost personified death in his great chapter on the resurrection, "Death is swallowed up in victory" (1 Cor. 15:54). John personified death when he wrote, "And the sea gave up the dead in it, Death and Hades gave up the dead in them, and all were judged by what they had done. Then Death and Hades were thrown into the lake of fire" (Rev. 20:13-14).

The reign of sin is also seen in the concept of slavery. Paul reminded the Romans that they "were once slaves of sin" (Rom. 6:17), but even though they "were slaves of sin" they were now free (v. 20). The concept that we are in slavery to sin and death speaks clearly of the reign of death.

The reign of death is also expressed in Ephesians in the words "when you were dead through the trespasses and sins in which you once walked" (Eph. 2:1-2). Death is not only an enemy but also a tyrant who has usurped power over our lives and reigns with ruthless tyranny.

Death as Destruction

Death is an enemy which destroys. Hebrew faith did not recognize other gods or hostile angels who could invade God's world with death as was the case in other religions. Death, however, becomes the destroying power in relation to man's sins. While mortality in the Bible is a characteristic of life, the curse resulting from sin makes death a destroying power.

When Paul wrote "the wages of sin is death" (Rom. 6:23), he spoke about the inevitable destruction of human life separated from God. Sin is the "sting of death" (1 Cor. 15:56).

Contemporary studies in ecology point out that the death of one type of plant or animal is part of the food chain which provides life to another. Death and decay provide the sustenance for new life. Typical faith regards human death in an entirely different way. Death is destruction. In death we are separated from life and possibly from God.

Death as the Wages of Sin

Paul wrote, "For the wages of sin is death, but the free gift of God is eternal life in Christ Jesus our Lord" (Rom. 6:23). Note that the contrast is between death and eternal life. An additional contrast is in the phrases "wages of sin" and "free gift of God." Eternal life is always regarded as a gift of God's grace and never something that we earn. Death on the other hand is considered the legitimate consequence of the life of sin.

This expression "wages of sin" stresses three ideas: (1) the inevitable connection between sin and death, (2) death is the just consequence of sin, (3) the free gift of God is eternal life through Jesus Christ.

Death, the Enemy of Jesus

Many Christians, thinking to do a high honor to Jesus, find subtle ways to deny His genuine humanity. Without knowing it, they fall into the early heresy of Docetism. These people cannot really accept the fact that Jesus was tempted. They find a way to rationalize around the temptation by assuming that Jesus really never could have thought about doing evil. Because of their reverence for Jesus, they tend to read over the stark statements of His humanity found in the New Testament. Nowhere is this more evident than in the event of Jesus' death.

On the night of Gethsemane Jesus urged His disciples to "sit here, while I pray" (Mark 14:32). Jesus was in agony. He stood in the shadow of death. He "took with him Peter and James and John, and began to be greatly distressed and troubled" (v. 33). Then he said to them, "My soul is very sorrowful, even to death; remain here, and watch" (v. 34). Then, Jesus prayed that if possible He might be spared death. In His prayer He said, "Abba, Father, all things are possible to thee; remove this cup from me; yet not what I will, but what thou

wilt" (v. 36). Again He pleaded with the disciples to watch and pray
(v. 37), and again He went and prayed (v. 39).

At the hour of Jesus' death, He cried out in sheer agony, "My God,
my God, why hast thou forsaken me?" (Mark 15:34). Oscar Cullman
insisted that even for Jesus death was a fearful encounter, an enemy
which destroyed and an experience of utter loneliness. Jesus did not
blithely walk through the experience of death as if it did not matter.
Rather, He went through the horror and loathsomeness of death to
save us. One cannot grasp the beauty of the resurrection without
grasping the horror of His death.[4]

The Last Enemy

We have noted the dreadful sorrow in which Jesus went to His own
death. We have noted that death is always an enemy. In the agony
which surrounds death, however, there is one bright ray of hope.
Death is the last enemy.

Jesus' death was followed by His resurrection. Paul explained this
resurrection as victory over death not only for Jesus Christ but also
for all of those who believed in Him. He uttered those encouraging
words, "The last enemy to be destroyed is death" (1 Cor. 15:26).

In His resurrection from the dead, Jesus destroyed death and the
power of death over His own life. When human beings hear the gospel
and believe in Jesus Christ, they also witness the destruction of their
death as the last enemy. John concluded his great drama of redemption as the destruction of sin, death, and the devil by his statement,
"then Death and Hades were thrown into the lake of fire" (Rev.
20:14). Facing death may be compared to the experience of a soldier
going into the last great battle of a war. He has known the dangers
of previous battles. He faces one more battle which in many ways is
worse than all of the others combined. There is, however, a major
difference. He can face the danger of this battle because of his conviction that it is the last battle and on the other side is victory.

Christian Views of Death

No attempt will be made in this section to deal comprehensively with all the views or statements about death in the New Testament. We will, however, look at some of the insights which help to form a Christian understanding of death.

Death as the Opposite of Life

The Christian view of death builds upon the Hebrew idea of death in the Old Testament. From the very beginning, the Hebrews thought of life as characterized by breath. The breath, which was the principle of life in creation, means considerably more than inhaling or exhaling. It is difficult to translate this term without some distortion. The view is much earlier than the Greek idea of the soul as a separate entity from the body. Breath in the Hebrew designates the principle of life or the animating force in life. It is quite natural since the cessation of breath means death.

Death then is the opposite of life. The absence of life is synonymous with death. Paul could comment that the Gentiles were dead through their trespasses in sins before they came to true life in Jesus Christ (Eph. 2:1). They were certainly alive biologically but they were not truly alive in the sense that people are who believe in God.

Nowhere is this contrast any more evident than in Paul's spiritual interpretation of baptism (Rom. 6:1-14). Paul argued that, since we have come to faith in Christ, we have "died to sin" and can no longer "live in it" (v. 2). Paul interpreted our immersion in baptism as being "baptized into Christ Jesus and therefore baptized into his death" (v. 3). "We were buried therefore with him by baptism into death, so that as Christ was raised from the dead by the glory of the Father, we too might walk in newness of life" (v. 4). Mysteriously, our experience of salvation in Christ pictured by baptism not only portrays Christ's death, burial, and resurrection but also portrays our death, burial, and resurrection.

We were "dead to sin," but now we are "alive to God in Christ Jesus" (v. 11). Obviously death here has little to do with biological death but has a great deal to do with true life and death as related to the spirit.

Death as Separation

Death, in the Old Testament, was a separation from life, the people of God, and, to an extent, God Himself even though Sheol was accessible to God. We experience grief at the time of the death of our loved ones because it means permanent separation. This separation not only designates their removal from our company but also designates the interruption of their lives in terms of what they were doing. Many of them were devoting their lives to causes which really matter. Death means that all of those good pursuits must be relinquished.

The understanding of death as separation is one basis for understanding the nature of hell, which will be discussed later. The parables on judgment stress a separation between the sheep and the goats, the good and the bad. The parable of the rich man and Lazarus portrays a separation that is permanent. The second death in Revelation 20:14 portrays an eternal separation. Those whose names are not written in the book of life, along with death, will be eternally separated from God, from all that is godly, and from all those who believe in God.

Death as Sleep

On several occasions in the New Testament, death is interpreted by the analogy of sleep. On one occasion a ruler came to Jesus reporting that his daughter had died. Jesus remarked, "The girl is not dead but sleeping" (Matt. 9:24). The same account appears in Mark 5. Jesus miraculously raised the dead but spoke of death as sleep. When Paul spoke about death and resurrection he said, "Lo! I tell you a mystery. We shall not all sleep, but we shall all be changed" (1 Cor. 15:51).

On another occasion when Paul was speaking about the Thessalonian Christians who had died, he spoke of them as "those who are asleep" (1 Thess. 4:13). When the New Testament writers spoke of death as sleep, they were not doing so as some moderns do in order to avoid the shocking reality of death. On the contrary, they were stressing their faith that physical death is not final, certainly not ultimate, that we shall rise in the resurrection. The comparison of death to sleep is a very natural comparison which actually needs no explanation.

Death as a Shadow Over Life

Even though we may not regard death as ultimate because we believe in the resurrection, we still live our lives under the shadow of death. For those who believe in God, the dark shadow of death may sometimes be the background against which we do our best living.

King Hezekiah is a good example. Hezekiah was sick to the point of death. The great prophet Isaiah had come and said to him, "Thus says the Lord: Set your house in order; for you shall die, you shall not recover" (Isa. 38:1). Perhaps you recall that Hezekiah wept bitterly and prayed to God who sent Isaiah back to Hezekiah to tell him that God would add fifteen years to Hezekiah's life. God gave Hezekiah a sign by making the shadow retreat on the sundial of King Ahaz.

King Hezekiah rededicated his life to God, as indicated in the song of the same chapter. Hezekiah found the true meaning of life with that encounter with death. He literally stood in the shadow of death and faced the horror. We should avoid reading this passage to people who are terminally ill if we mean to promise them that God will do the same miracle for them that He did for Hezekiah. We can learn from this parable, however, that the quality of living may be greatly enhanced under the awareness or the threat of death.

According to tradition, Paul was in jail in Rome when he wrote the letter to Timothy that appears in 2 Timothy 4:6-8. Evidently Paul was already under the sentence of death which would lead to his execution by the Ostian Road outside the city of Rome as his Lord had been put to death outside the north wall of Jerusalem. Paul wrote,

> I am already on the point of being sacrificed; the time of my departure has come. I have fought the good fight, I have finished the race, I have kept the faith. Henceforth there is laid up for me the crown of righteousness, which the Lord, the righteous judge, will award to me on

that Day, and not only to me, but also to all who have loved his appearing.

Life cannot be measured merely by weeks and months and years. Rather, life is measured by our faithfulness to God and God's people. In the shadow of death, Paul's life was at its fullest.

Death as a Vanquished Enemy

We have noted previously that death often appears as a personified enemy. We see the picture of a skeleton heavily robed holding a scythe in his hands waiting in the shadows. This enemy is never far away.

The death and resurrection of Jesus Christ became the victory over death and its companion sin. A great portrait of that victory appears at the close of the final judgment when "Death and Hades were thrown into the lake of fire" (Rev. 20:14).

Death as a New Beginning

In the joy of our hope for the resurrection from the dead, we are tempted to speak too lightly about death. In trying to comfort the grieving, Christians often make statements about death which border on triviality.

When we deal with our hope of the resurrection, we are also tempted to minimize the seriousness of death. Some interpreters speak of death as a mere transition from this life to the next. Perhaps it would not be erroneous to compare death to one of the passages of life. Can we say that we move from infancy, to and through childhood, adolescence, adulthood, old age, and death to a new beginning? One interpreter concluded his study of death with the following statement: "In short, for the Christian, death interrupts nothing; it destroys nothing; it liberates, not from the body, but from the empire of sin."[5]

I cannot agree that death interrupts nothing and destroys nothing. It interrupts almost everything, and it destroys what it touches. Nor can I agree that death liberates from the empire of sin. In my judgment, Jesus Christ's death and resurrection and our faith in Him liberates from sin. Nothing else does.

I have heard tourists who have visited Europe since World War II speak of the marvelous rebuilding of the German cities. Some rather flippantly remark that the nation is better off than it would have been without the destruction. There is something very shallow about such an observation. We shall come nearer to understanding death if we take more seriously its pain and agony and grieve with those people who, in the late 1930s and early 1940s, witnessed the destruction not only of what they had built and inherited but also of their families. It also follows that we should express gratitude for those who have the courage to rise up from the ashes.

The Place of the Dead

There is a gap between individual death and the final resurrection. The human mind cannot be reconciled to an empty gap. Since people cannot fathom a gap in time, or a time of nothingness, they ask, "Where are the dead?" The fact is, we have very little information on that subject. It is entirely possible that the biblical writers did not intend for us to produce a calendar on which we list in sequence all of the events following death. It is just possible that after death we enter the eternal dimension where time and sequence are not important, or do not exist at all, as we now know them. It is also possible that we have projected our limited time view into eternity.

People still ask the question, however, and others provide numerous answers.[6]

Sheol and Hades

The Old Testament idea of Sheol, the place or the realm of the dead, appears to be translated in the New Testament by the idea of Hades. (See Matt. 11:23; 16:18; Luke 10:15; 16:23; Acts 2:27, 31; Rev. 1:18; 6:8; 20:13-14.)

An Intermediate (Interim) State

Theologians commonly affirm a kind of existence between death and the final consummation. Most often this interim state is divided into two sections: Paradise for the righteous, and Hades for the wicked.

The passages most often cited as teaching such an interim place or state are: (1) the story of the rich man and Lazarus in Luke 16:19-31; (2) Jesus' statement to the thief on the cross, "Truly, I say unto you, today you will be with me in Paradise" (Luke 23:43); (3) Paul's passage about the disembodied spirit in 1 Corinthians 5:1-8; (4) Paul's statement about the man who was caught up into the third heaven about whom he said, "I know that this man was caught up into Paradise—whether in the body or out of the body I do not know" (2 Cor. 12:2-3); (5) Paul's statement in Philippians 1:23 that his desire was "to depart and be with Christ, for that is far better"; and (6) the passage in 1 Peter 3:19 about Jesus after the crucifixion going and preaching "to the spirits in prison."

Paradise of Luke 23 would be an intermediate state. On the basis of Paul's statement in Philippians 1:23 and the description of the poor man in paradise of Luke 16, this place or state would be preferable to life on earth. On the basis of the same passages, many Christians believe that the departed saints are both alive and conscious, at rest, and blessed in the presence of the Lord. On the other hand, the wicked are in prison or under restraint as suggested by 1 Peter 3:19. They are in a state of torment or conscious suffering as indicated in Luke 16:23. Sometimes, 2 Peter 2:9 is quoted to show that they are under punishment.[7]

Ray Summers discussed this theme under the heading "The Disembodied State."[8] He defined this disembodied state as "the conscious existence of both the righteous and the wicked after death and prior to the resurrection."[9] On the basis of the passages cited, he concluded that in this interim state the righteous are (1) with God, (2) in paradise, (3) alive and conscious, and (4) at rest. He insisted that it is a conscious state, a fixed state, and an incomplete state in that it awaits the final resurrection.

Summers taught that the wicked are (1) separated from God, (2) alive and conscious, (3) under punishment, (4) at a fixed place and that they, too, are in a conscious state which is fixed but incomplete awaiting their final condemnation. My teacher, Professor Dale Moody, had a very helpful survey of the "intermediate state"[10] in which he gave documentation of those theologians who taught about the intermediate state. For instance, Augustine spoke about the souls of men being reserved in secret storehouses either at rest or in tribulation awaiting the final judgment.

The intermediate state should be distinguished from purgatory. Purgatory is a particular view of an intermediate state where people can either improve their lot or have their lot improved for them by the prayers and sacrifices of the living on their behalf. I know of no biblical basis for the doctrine of purgatory. The nearest evidence that I know is a statement from 2 Maccabees in which Judas Maccabaeus offered prayers on behalf of the dead who had fallen in battle presumably because they wore good luck charms around their necks violating the Commandment about images.

The view of an interim or intermediate state should also be distinguished from "soul sleeping" which has been popularized in recent times. Apparently Martin Luther believed that at death we simply go to sleep and remain there until the final resurrection when God will awaken us.[11]

The Mystery of Death

We know very little about the realm of the dead. After the resurrection, Jesus gave no lectures which have survived on what happened there. Quite naturally we build mental images of what is beyond. Some ancient people thought of the realm of the dead as a cavern under the earth, probably suggested by their practice of burying the dead in caves. The view of the underworld was quite natural because of graves dug in the ground. Those images are less satisfying to us today because of our knowledge of what is under the ground.

A popular story compares death to the departure of a ship. We stand watching while the sails are unfurled, and the ship moves away with the wind. In time it becomes only a white speck of canvas on the horizon. Then it appears to be totally gone. The departure of the dead appears in that way and they appear to be "gone." But it appears that way because of our position on this side of the ocean. If we could imagine some days or weeks later, people standing on the distant shore on the other side see the white sails of the ship, then the ship, which finally docks in the harbor. It is not completely "gone" as it appeared to be.

The mystery of death remains, but the resurrection gives us hope beyond.

Death with No Beyond

Christians who believe in life after death need to remember that many of their contemporaries do not. They also need to remember that some contemporaries apparently do not shudder at the thought of death. Years ago I read a volume by William Ernest Hocking.[12] He reasoned that death does not have to be a major calamity and that we can see our own death as a passing to make room for others to live in the world, to allow for the flexibility and change in history which is possible under new leadership but which would be impossible under old leadership.

Hocking argued that when you and I face the reality that we, too, shall die, we come to realize for the first time the nature of time and of life. He reasoned that if we had endless time to squander on every task before us we would never know the importance of now. The limitation of time, which is clearest in the awareness of death, imposes an urgency and a seriousness upon each moment.

He also reasoned that genuine freedom can be known only if we learn that we need not live forever. The willingness to die or the acceptance of death makes genuine freedom possible. He pictured human beings desperately clinging to life and unwilling to take the risks which normal people take. The great things in life are done by those who are willing to die. We pay tribute to those brave people who without a view of resurrection and eternal life find meaning and joy in this life and in death. We, however, believe that we have been shown a more excellent way through the resurrection of Jesus Christ from the dead.

Notes

1. Emil Brunner, *Eternal Hope,* Harold Knight, trans. (Philadelphia: The Westminster Press, 1954), p. 97.

2. Loraine Boettner, *Immortality* (London: Pickering and Inglis, Ltd., 1958), p. 16.

3. John Baillie, *And the Life Everlasting* (London: Oxford University Press, 1934), p. 53-54.

4. Oscar Cullman, *Immortality of the Soul or Resurrection of the Dead?* (London: The Epworth Press, 1958), p. 27.

5. Robert Gleason, *The World to Come* (London: Sheed and Ward, 1959), p. 77.

6. Boettner, pp. 91-159.

7. Augustus Hawkins Strong, *Systematic Theology* (Philadelphia: The Judson Press, 1907), pp. 998-1003.

8. Ray Summers, *The Life Beyond* (Nashville: Broadman Press, 1959), pp. 15-29.

9. Ibid.

10. Dale Moody, *The Hope of Glory* (Grand Rapids: William B. Eerdmans Publishing Company, 1964), pp. 67-77.

11. Ibid.

12. William Ernest Hocking, *The Meaning of Immortality in Human Experience* (New York: Harper & Brothers Publishers, 1957), pp. 10 *ff.*

4

Hope and the Resurrection

From that time Jesus began to show His disciples that he must go to Jerusalem and suffer many things from the elders and chief priests and scribes, and be killed, and on *the third day* be raised (Matt. 16:21, author's italics).

For I delivered to you as of first importance what I also received, that Christ died for our sins in accordance with the scriptures, that he was buried, and that he was raised on *the third day* in accordance with the scriptures (1 Cor. 15:3-4, author's italics).

The Foundation of Our Resurrection-Hope

In these passages we note both the prediction and the fulfillment that Christ would rise on the third day. This striking reference to the calendar appears in several places, drawing our attention to the specific and historical nature of Christ's resurrection.

Jesus Predicted His Resurrection

Matthew and Luke (9:22; 18:33; 24:7) used the phrase "the third day." Mark (8:31; 9:31; 10:34) used the phrase "after three days." Apparently months before the crucifixion, Jesus recognized that His death was inevitable and that His death and resurrection would be important in His saving work. Obviously the disciples did not understand this fully in light of their behavior at the time of the crucifixion.

Jesus shared the Hebrew belief in the resurrection from the dead, as indicated in the account of Lazarus. When Martha said to Jesus

"Lord, if you had been here, my brother would not have died," Jesus replied, "Your brother will rise again in the resurrection at the last day." Jesus added a statement, "I am the resurrection and the life; he who believes in me, though he die, yet shall he live, and whoever lives and believes in me shall never die" (John 11:21, 23, 25-26).

Jesus' statements about the resurrection, as recorded in the Gospels, are revealing in these areas: (1) He indicated the acceptance of the Hebrew belief in a general resurrection at the last day; (2) He specified that His own resurrection would be on the third day after the crucifixion, quite different from the last day; and (3) He claimed that He embodied the resurrection in His own person.

Some interpreters attribute these statements to someone other than Jesus and a generation after the resurrection. The evidence is strong that the predictions are Jesus' own statements. Also, the nature of the Fourth Gospel fully justifies Jesus' statement that He was the resurrection. Both the embodiment and the present time of the resurrection are quite consistent with the Gospel of John.

Jesus' prediction and the New Testament emphasis on the resurrection show its centrality in the Christian faith.

He Arose on the Third Day

In Chapter 2 we noted the evidence supporting the conviction that Jesus was, in fact, raised from the dead. It was presented at that point to answer the question, "Why do we Christians have a hope in resurrection from the dead and for life everlasting?" I will not repeat, nor even summarize, but suggest that the reader refer to those pages.[1]

The Foundation of Our Hope

Paul reasoned,

But if there is no resurrection of the dead, then Christ has not been raised; if Christ has not been raised, then our preaching is in vain and your faith is in vain. If Christ has not been raised, your faith is futile and you are still in your sins. Then those also who have fallen asleep in Christ have perished. But in fact Christ has been raised from the dead, the first fruits of those who have fallen asleep. For as by a man came death, by a man has come also the resurrection of the dead (1 Cor. 15:13-14, 17-18, 20-21).

The New Testament speaks in other places about the resurrection of Jesus being the foundation of our belief in our resurrection, but the fifteenth chapter of 1 Corinthians is the most complete discussion of the subject in the New Testament.

In this passage: (1) Paul was refuting the idea that there is no resurrection; (2) if Christ was not raised, then our preaching and salvation are in vain (without foundation); (3) we are false witnesses because we (Christians) have been proclaiming the gospel of the resurrection; (4) if Christ was not raised, we are still in our sins; (5) if Christ was not raised, believers who have died have perished; (6) but, Christ has been raised; (7) His resurrection is the basis of our belief in the resurrection; and, (8) the universality of sin known among the descendants of Adam is now parallel to the certitude of the resurrection achieved for us through Christ, the second Adam. Our hope in the resurrection from the dead is as sure as the resurrection of Jesus.

The idea of the resurrection from the dead did not originate with Jesus. The Pharisees held to the belief in the resurrection during Jesus' lifetime. It was already a widely accepted view, even though the Sadducees did not accept it. The prophet Daniel (12:2) had written of a general resurrection including both the righteous and the wicked.

The resurrection of Jesus established this belief by being the historical manifestation before witnesses. The Christian gospel does not cite a general belief but a specific event as its basis for teaching the resurrection hope in our future. "The resurrection of Jesus is the foundation stone of the entire New Testament witness."[2] Because He was raised, we believe that we also shall be raised.

The Third Day Becomes the First Day

The promise that Jesus would be raised on the third day inspires hope. The fulfillment of that promise undergirds all of our hope for the future. In fact, it was so important that, in a sense, we can refer to it as "The First Day" of Christian faith. That first day is "The Lord's Day."

The Dawning of the New Age

The Reality of the Resurrection

"Now after the sabbath, toward the dawn of *the first day* of the week, Mary Magdalene and the other Mary went to see the sepulchre." But, an angel of the Lord announced "He is not here; for he has risen, as he said. Come, see the place where he lay" (Matt. 28: 1, 6, author's italics). This simple notation of the date and time when Mary Magdalene and the other Mary went to the tomb unwittingly included two terms of great importance in Christian faith: "the *dawn*," and "*the first day* of the week."

The events of that first day of the week so established the faith of the Christians that they changed their day of worship from the Hebrew sabbath to the first day of the week which became known as the Lord's Day. Every Sunday became a celebration of the resurrection—a weekly celebration of Easter. This change in the calendar is incidental when compared to the importance of the resurrection.

The dawn is a mere notation of time in this statement, but in the event of the resurrection a new age had dawned.

The Dawning of the New Age

Hebrew hope included a Messiah whose coming would bring a new age. Their literature spoke often of these two ages: the present evil age, and the age to come. The resurrection of Jesus marks the beginning of the new age. We shall look at three examples: Paul's gospel, Peter's gospel, and some statements of Jesus.

Paul's gospel.—Paul did not preach a different gospel from that of the other Christian preachers. In fact, he was the quickest to deny that there was any other gospel (Gal. 1:7). But, Paul gave us our earliest written form of the gospel. He proclaimed that Jesus' resurrection marked the dawning of a new age.

Paul wrote the Galatians that Jesus gave Himself "to deliver us from the present evil age" (Gal. 1:4).[3] Paul was drawing upon his Hebrew tradition of the two ages. In Christ's death and resurrection, the boundary of the new age had been crossed. The new age acknowledges the lordship of Christ which also is seen in the resurrection (Rom. 8:9). The central theme of the gospel Paul preached was the death and resurrection of Christ which mark the change from this present evil age to the age to come. Paul believed the Hebrew prophets' declaration about the Day of the Lord had dawned in Christ.

Christ was raised from the dead, exalted above all rule and authority, and above every name, "not only in this age but also in that which is to come" (Eph. 1:21-22).

Although our Christian hope still looks forward to the coming of Christ and eternal life which will be a new age, in one sense, we join with Paul in seeing that in the resurrection of Christ a new age did begin.

Peter's gospel.—The early chapters of Acts record four speeches or sermons by Peter. Peter preached that the new age had dawned in Jesus Christ. He introduced his sermon by pointing out that what he would say about Christ had been "spoken by the prophet Joel" (Acts 2:16). He proceeded to speak of Jesus of Nazareth who had done mighty works, was killed, and was raised. Peter went on to quote David and related the fulfillment to the "resurrection of the Christ" (Acts 2:31). In Acts 3:18 and 24 Peter indicated God's speaking through the prophets about Christ. The messianic age has dawned in Christ.

In these sermons, Peter offered the forgiveness of sins in the name of Jesus who had been crucified and raised. The exaltation of Christ led to the statement that there was "no other name" by which we can be saved (Acts 4:12).

The new age began in the gospel of Christ. The clearest insight into the "Christian" gospel is in Peter's sermon to those who crucified Christ (Acts 2:22-23) whom he addressed and accused in the words "this Jesus whom you crucified" (v. 36). The remarkable Christian thing is that he immediately offered forgiveness to those who had committed the crime (v. 38). This is the Christian gospel, salvation through the cross for those who crucified Christ. The new age had begun.

Jesus' teaching.—When speaking about sinning against the Holy Spirit, Jesus said the guilty person would not be forgiven "either in this age or in the age to come" (Matt. 12:32). He may have been speaking of the last age to come or eternal life, as He was when He said "in the age to come eternal life" (Mark. 10:30).

When a man approached Jesus asking about eternal life (Mark 10:17), Jesus equated eternal life with having "treasure in heaven" (v. 21). He went on in the following verses (23-25) to make this the same as entrance into the kingdom. Then He spoke of the "age to come eternal life" (v. 30). It is obvious that the passage points to a future fulfillment of something that is already present.

The Resurrection Gospel of the New Age

Christian faith emerged in response to the life, teaching, death, and resurrection of Jesus Christ. This unique cluster of events marked the new age. Paul spoke of it as happening in a fullness of the time (Gal. 4:4). All history had been leading up to it. In this new age, the Spirit of God enters our hearts and we are now able to address God as "Abba! Father!"

The mystery of the cross was revealed in Jesus' resurrection. The early Christians were so marvelously reconciled to God in these events that they declared what had happened everywhere they went. This proclamation, which we call the gospel ("good news") was the very "power of God for salvation to every one who has faith, to the Jew first and also to the Greek" (Rom. 1:16). It was, indeed, a new age which removed racial distinctions and made all humanity one in Christ. The Epistle to the Ephesians states this unity most beautifully (4:1-7).

The gospel was stated rather briefly and plainly. Paul stated it succinctly in his great resurrection chapter. "For I delivered to you as of first importance what I also received, that *Christ died for our sins in accordance with the scriptures,* that *he was buried,* that *he was raised on the third day in accordance with the scriptures,* and that *he ap-*

peared" (1 Cor. 15:3-5, author's italics). The cross and resurrection are central.

Peter also placed the resurrection of Jesus in the center of the gospel. He wrote, "By his great mercy we have been born anew to a living hope through the resurrection of Jesus Christ from the dead, and to an inheritance which is imperishable, undefiled, and unfading, kept in heaven for you" (1 Pet. 1:3-4).

The most obvious implication of Jesus' resurrection is that it establishes our hope for a resurrection. It is even more significant that the resurrection of Jesus proves the meaning of the crucifixion, thereby providing a foundation for every Christian belief and affirmation. "The fact of the Resurrection is, then, the foundation stone of Christianity, even as it gave ultimate meaning to Our Lord's whole life."[4]

The Resurrection as a Present Reality

The eschatological themes of Christian doctrine often have both a present and a future orientation. We noted that one danger is neglecting either aspect. The resurrection appears at first to be completely a future hope. Further examination of the New Testament, however, convinces us that the resurrection is also a reality of the present moment for individual believers.

Two basic ideas are involved: (1) The resurrection is a quality of the present life as well as a future hope; (2) the hope of the future resurrection adds a quality to life in which the expectation, of itself, becomes a living reality.

Already resurrected.—The clearest statement of this theme is Paul's interpretation of the meaning of baptism. In short, Paul believed and taught that our experience of repentance and faith in Christ was a radical transformation of life so that we can speak accurately of the "old self" being "crucified" with Christ, "buried" with Christ, and already "raised" with him. The meaning of baptism, immersion in water, is that just as Christ was crucified, buried, and raised, so we, too, die to our sins, are buried with Christ, and are "raised" to "walk in newness of life" (Rom. 6:3-11).

Resurrection hope.—Belief in the future resurrection endows life with a joyful anticipation which brightens every day. The future resurrection-hope is like a magnet, drawing us and uplifting life in every dimension. We have already been "born anew" by this resurrection from the dead (1 Pet. 1:3). We have seen the "first fruits" and anticipate the harvest (1 Cor. 15:20; Col. 1:18: Rev. 1:5). We already have the guarantee of the Holy Spirit (2 Cor. 1:22; 5:5).

Heaven has begun.—We have just noted that the resurrection is a present reality for individuals. In a real sense, the resurrection life has begun in the community life. The church is the resurrection community now. The new covenant is no longer future; it is a present event. The kingdom of God, while a future hope, is now a present reality because of Jesus' resurrection from the dead.

Indeed, we await the fullness of life with God in heaven, but heaven has already begun in this life. There is a distinction between the third day and the last day, but we live in what Neville Clark has called "The Overlap of the Ages."[5] The disappointment which grew out of the delay in Christ's coming gave way to the awareness that the kingdom had come. People were being born anew, forgiven, reconciled to God and to each other. The church was a community of saints seeking to give the gospel to all persons and to include them in the family of God. We wait, but the future has invaded our present; the future kingdom already exercises the authority of our King. We celebrate the Lord's Supper as a messianic banquet as if the end of the age had already come.

The Future Resurrection

As Christian believers, we hold to a serious view of death. We do not look upon death with joy because we believe this life is a gift of God to be lived in faith, hope, and love with God and persons. We believe that the Christian life is a kind of resurrection life even now, but it is partial and incomplete. We live in a joyful hope that for us individually and for humanity as a whole there will be a resurrection at the last day.

The Thessalonian Question

The Christians in Thessalonica had clearly understood the belief that they would have eternal life. At least some of them had assumed that Jesus would return before their deaths. When some of their members died, they were confused. They sent a messenger to Paul, asking about death, the return of Christ, and the resurrection.

Paul responded to their question with the magnificent paragraph in one of the earliest writings of the New Testament. His First Epistle to the Thessalonians should be dated about AD 49 or 50. He spoke of their deceased loved ones as "asleep." He urged them not to grieve "as others do who have no hope." He reminded them of his and their hope, "For since we believe that Jesus died and rose again, even so, through Jesus, God will bring with him those who have fallen asleep" (1 Thess. 4:13-14).

Paul claimed that his answer was "by the word of the Lord." Seemingly Paul hoped that Jesus would return during the lifetime of his own generation because he wrote "that we who are alive, who are left until the coming of the Lord" will have no precedence over the dead (v. 15).

The question was not about the priority of the living over the dead. Paul's answer could conceivably give some preference to the deceased, but that is not the point. Paul's answer was one of assurance to living and dead that both would participate in the resurrection.

Paul answered that we will all share in the resurrection. He indicated that Christ will return, raise the "dead in Christ," and then those of us still living. Our common destiny is to "meet the Lord in the air" and to be always "with the Lord" (vv. 16-17). Regrettably, people analyze the paragraph determined to establish a sequence and priority for the events that will attend the coming of Christ. Even more regrettable, I feel, is the fact that many come to the text with their preconceived scheme and force the text into their outline, even separating it to make room for other events not mentioned.

Paul's entire answer breathes the spirit stated in the last sentence, "Therefore comfort one another with these words" (v. 18). The great affirmations of hope, the return of Christ, the resurrection of the dead, the meeting of all believers both living and dead with the Lord, and our eternal abode with Him, issue in the assuring word that we face both life and death with this hope. Whether we are still alive when the Lord comes or whether we have long since departed doesn't really matter. In either case, we shall be charter members of the resurrection.

Our Hope of a Future Resurrection

On the basis of Jesus' resurrection from the dead, we have a strong hope that we, too, will be raised with Him. We need to note at least two themes that will be discussed a little later. The hope for the resurrection is twofold: (1) Hope is related to individual destiny, and (2) hope includes all humanity, a cosmic event.

Each person has every reason to think of his or her own resurrection from the dead, individual destiny. Each, however, needs to beware of letting this hope become self-centered at the expense of losing sight of all other persons.

The cosmic event of the resurrection must be seen, also, as the raising of the individual persons who form humanity. It would deny God's purpose in creation to think of a final consummation in so general or cosmic a sense that individuals lose their identity. We believe that in the resurrection we will have the capacity to love all of God's creatures and be saved from our selfishness.

We stand with the Christians of all ages who included in their creeds and confessions some statement like "we believe in the resurrection of the dead," or "we believe in the resurrection of the body."

The Nature of the Resurrection-Hope

A number of ideas about the nature of the resurrection-hope have been implied. A brief summary will be adequate at this time. It will focus on the questions asked most often about the resurrection.

The Questions

When will we be raised?—This question usually voices a hope that there will be no delay, or intermediate state, between individual death and the resurrection. We have briefly looked at this issue in Chapter 3.

The Thessalonian question also provided insight into this discussion. Paul's response focused on the fact, or promise, of the resurrection and related it to the coming of Christ and did not specify much about the *when.* Also involved in the *when* is the matter of individual destiny and cosmic resurrection discussed previously.

What kind of resurrection body?—This question prompted Paul's lengthy discussion in 1 Corinthians 15. We shall look at it in more detail later in this section.

What will resurrection life be like?—While the most complete discussion of this question will have to wait till our last chapter on heaven, I will suggest, in a preliminary way, some aspects of this life in a short time. First, we need to look at some inadequate and incorrect answers which may interfere with our getting a clear answer.

Inadequate and Incorrect Answers

Not mere perpetuity.—Resurrection from the dead does not result in mere perpetuity. The ancients believed in ghostly survival, which was a gloomy prospect. Christians believe that life is a gift from God to be enjoyed. Whatever else the resurrection may be, it does not mean merely duration, endless duration. Rather, it means everlasting life in a new sense with a new meaning.

Not totally new.—When we speak of a new creation, we speak of a transformation. The resurrection of Jesus leads us to expect a change, but it also requires continuity. We shall be changed, but we shall be a continuation. The resurrection life will be a fulfillment of life, not a totally new construction.

Not a human achievement or conquest.—We shall avoid much error if we remember that *God* gave us life and raises us from the dead. Eternal life is a gift from God. It is not, therefore, an achievement of men or women. Neither is it a reward which would be an achievement. It is a work of God.

The desire for a resurrection and eternal life could be merely another selfish ambition of human beings. A rich young man came to Jesus and said something like, "Rumor has it that you know about eternal life. I have everything else. If you know, tell me. I want it too. I could even pay for it." He went away sorrowful because, in his self-centeredness, he could not know God.

Since God raises us from the dead, it seems certain that the life which follows will be on a higher level than this life and, in a sense, a fulfillment of God's purpose for us as well as our hope.

The Resurrection Body

The creeds and confessions always speak of the "resurrection of the body" or the "resurrection of the flesh." In so doing, they witness to the importance of the belief in the resurrection. They intended to insist that Jesus was really dead and that the same Jesus was raised. They also meant to insist that when we are raised we will be the same persons transformed, not totally different persons. We do not easily understand why they said it the way they did.

We have noted several times that the biblical view of human life is quite different from that of Greek philosophy. In particular, the immortality of the soul differs from the Christian belief in the resurrection. If this distinction is not clear, it will be difficult to understand what Paul meant by the bodily resurrection.[6]

We have two major insights into the question of the resurrection body: Jesus' resurrection body, and Paul's discussion of the subject.

Jesus' resurrection body.—Mystery surrounds the appearances of Jesus after the resurrection. We must be cautious not to say more than the evidence suggests.

Jesus was recognizable. The disciples saw Him (Luke 24:39-40) and recognized such details as hands and feet. He ate fish with them (v. 43). They could touch Him. These details convinced them and us that Jesus had been raised. He was the same Jesus.

Jesus was different, however. The witnesses reported that He seemed to appear somewhat independent of the usual space and time limits. He entered through a closed door, for instance (John 20:19,26). Sometimes the disciples could not recognize Him, as in the case of the two on the way to Emmaus (Luke 24:16).

The evidence suggests beyond doubt that Jesus had been raised. He was different, however, in that many of the human limits were no longer evident. He was not pure spirit, however, unless we assume that He could somehow manage to appear in some visible form. The disciples were not hindered by modern concepts of psychology or physiology. They were convinced that their Lord, the man Jesus, the person, had been transformed from a life subject to death to life beyond death.

Paul's discussion of bodily resurrection.—Apparently someone in Corinth was denying the resurrection. Paul's response was the assurance of the fact of the resurrection and a discussion of "How are the dead raised? With what kind of body do they come?" (1 Cor 15:35). The response stresses that (1) death and resurrection may be compared to a kernel of grain which "dies" and germinates; (2) we see a great variety of bodies, so God is able to give us a bodily existence after the resurrection; (3) the resurrection of a person is a great transformation; (4) our bodily existence after the resurrection will be characterized by the "spiritual" body rather than by the physical.

Paul used four words when speaking about our human existence: *flesh, body, soul,* and *spirit.*[7] All of these are related to what we call human personality. Flesh is the physical structure of our existence. Body is not only physical body but also full personality. Soul is the life principle in us. Spirit relates us to God who is Spirit. These are not different entities, but rather, aspects of the single entity of human personality.

The resurrection body is like the new plant which emerges from the seed. In speaking of mysteries, we often resort to comparisons. Everyone has marvelled at the life process of the germinating seed. Paul reasoned that death and resurrection of human life would be like this. The mystery of life is hidden in the seed that "dies" from which springs a new life. The seed, however, "died" but was not totally destroyed. The seed included within itself a destiny as mysterious as the full-grown plant. The seed was raised to new life by a combination of moisture and warmth from the sun.

Paul argued, by analogy, that our destiny is eternal life with God. We die. God raises us up. Our new existence is a spiritual bodily existence.[8]

When Paul spoke of different kinds of bodies, such as human, animal, earthly, and heavenly bodies, he was opening the imagination of the mind to accept the variety that is already obvious. We should be able to accept the belief that God, who has provided this great variety of existence, is capable of giving us a real existence in the resurrection.

The emphasis of Paul is upon the great transformation in which we become imperishable, glorious, and powerful. We shall have been fully restored to God and elevated to the destiny which God had in mind for us.

The "spiritual body" is an affirmation, not a denial. To Paul there was no existence except bodily existence. He did not despise the flesh as the later Gnostics did. Paul knew the limitations of the flesh. He did not think the resurrection body would be one of "flesh and blood" (v. 50), but he thought the resurrection body would be the human personality whom God had created and placed on this earth for preparation and had now raised to his or her destiny.

In Pauline thought the contrast between things "of the flesh" and things "of the Spirit" does not despise human earthly existence. That contrast was between two types of human life, one which lives dominated by carnal appetites "according to the flesh," and the other who lives motivated by the things of God, "according to the Spirit" (Rom. 8:5).

The resurrection body will be God's creation in which He preserves the human personality in its highest form. This existence will be a glorious transformation, but it will maintain continuity with the earthly life. Each of us is already the creature of God whom God cherishes. Our distinctive personhood is infinitely more precious to Him than even to our dearest loved ones.

"Beloved, we are God's children now; it does not yet appear what we shall be, but we know that when he appears *we shall be like him,* for we shall see him as he is" (1 John 3:2, author's italics).

Notes

1. See pages 26-33. For further discussions about the resurrection of Jesus see, "Resurrection" articles in Bible dictionaries; George Eldon Ladd, *I Believe in the Resurrection of Jesus* (Grand Rapids: William B. Eerdmans Publishing Company, 1975); C. F. Evans, *Resurrection and the New Testament* (Naperville, Ill.: Alec R. Allenson Inc., 1970).

2. Neville Clark, *Interpreting the Resurrection* (Philadelphia: The Westminster Press, 1967), p. 44.

3. For a complete discussion of the New Testament emphasis that Christ brought the new age, see C. H. Dodd, *The Apostolic Preaching and Its Development* (London: Hodder & Stoughton Limited, 1936), pp. 11 *ff.*

4. Robert Gleason, *The World to Come* (London: Sheed and Ward, 1959), p. 133.

5. Clark, pp. 72-80.

6. See Oscar Cullmann, *Immortality of the Soul or Resurrection of the Dead?* (London: The Epworth Press, 1958); Anthony A. Hoekema, *The Bible and the Future* (Grand Rapids: William B. Eerdmans Publishing Company, 1979), pp. 239 *ff.;* Murray J. Harris, *Raised Immortal, Resurrection and Immortality in the New Testament* (Grand Rapids: William B. Eerdmans Publishing Company, 1983).

7. Thomas S. Kepler, *The Meaning and Mystery of the Resurrection* (New York: Association Press, 1963), p. 106.

8. M. E. Dahl, *The Resurrection of the Body* (London: SCM Press Ltd., 1962), pp. 15 *ff.*

5

Hope and the Return of Christ

In my Father's house are many mansions: if it were not so, I would
have told you. I go to prepare a place for you. And if I go and prepare
a place for you, I will come again, and receive you unto myself; that
where I am, there ye may be also (John 14:2-3, KJV).

And just as it is appointed for men to die once, and after that comes
judgment, so Christ, having been offered once to bear the sins of many,
will appear a second time, not to deal with sin but to save those who
are eagerly waiting for him (Heb. 9:27-28).

Faith in Jesus Christ without the expectation of His Parousia is a
voucher that is never redeemed, a promise that is not seriously meant.
A Christian faith without expectation of the Parousia is like a ladder
which leads nowhere but ends in the void.[1]

Jesus' promise of John 14 led to the expectation expressed in Hebrews 9. The early Christians cherished a hope that Christ who had
lived among them and had been snatched away by the crucifixion
would come again. That expectation of Christ's return became an
important element in Christian eschatology and continues to be so, as
indicated by the preceding quotation from theologian Emil Brunner.

Terminology and Definition

The Greek word *Parousia* is the primary term used in the New
Testament to indicate Christ's return, and it is often used without
translation as the title of this eschatological theme. The word *Parousia*
literally means "presence" or "being with." In light of Jesus' depar-

ture, to speak of His presence came to mean His return, or coming again.

Several other words are used in the New Testament to designate the same belief. Examples are the "day of our Lord Jesus Christ" (1 Cor 1:8), the "days of the Son of man" (Luke 17:22), "revealing" (1 Cor. 1:7), "appear" (Col. 3:4; 1 Pet 5:4; 1 John 2:28), and "appearing" (2 Thess. 2:8).

While the word *Parousia,* and the other words as well, often mean merely presence or appearing, they designated the expectation of a future presence or coming. In popular usage, this belief is usually entitled "the second coming" or "the second advent." This exact expression does not appear in the New Testament, but is a natural interpretation in light of the passages cited. The term *second coming* is suitable, but I prefer to use the biblical term *Parousia* or coming.

This brief review indicates the variety of terms and the frequency of their appearance in the New Testament. The early Christians spoke quite naturally of their belief that Jesus Christ would come again. Reference to Jesus' Parousia could mean a kind of spiritual presence only. The New Testament evidence, however, insists on a coming in relation to the end of history. We are left with many uncertainties, but we are sure of one thing: Christ's *Parousia* is not synonymous with the doctrine of the Holy Spirit's presence now.

The Priority Of Christ's First Coming

In the world influenced by Christian thought, we construct our calendars by dating events BC or AD. The belief that Jesus Christ is the center of history leads quite naturally to the belief that Jesus Christ is related to all history and, therefore, will figure prominently in the end of history.

Jesus Christ marked a radical new beginning in world history. We Christians treasure our historical and religious heritage with the Hebrew people. We accept with gratitude the Hebrew Bible as a part of the Christian Bible. The Hebrew Law, Prophets, and Writings have shaped our faith. The coming of Christ, however, inspired a new pilgrimage and tradition.

We believe that God was active in Israel's history and religion. Her worship is our worship, but there is a difference. In a unique sense, "In Christ God was reconciling the world to himself" (2 Cor. 5:19). This incarnation of God in Christ fulfilled and surpassed all of Israel's hopes. Jesus Christ broke the bonds of a national religion and included the whole world in His work of reconciliation.

We believe that Jesus Christ is the Word of God Incarnate (John 1:14), the "image of the invisible God" (Col. 1:15) in whom the "fulness of God was pleased to dwell" (v. 19), and He bore "the very stamp" of God's nature (Heb. 1:3).

All Christian beliefs are shaped by our belief that God came into the world in the person of Jesus Christ. We understand the Old Testament as preparatory and preliminary to the coming of Christ. Jesus Christ determines our doctrine of God and, hence, of the Holy Spirit. Since Christ is the Alpha and Omega of Christian faith, His coming in the incarnation would chart the course for our interpretation of His expected return. So, we understand His second coming in terms of His first coming.[2]

The Promise and the Expectation of Christ's Return

The New Testament scholars differ widely on the interpretation of those statements about Christ's return, the end of the age, and the Day of the Lord.[3] We are not able to discern with certainty whether Jesus spoke of the end of the age or the destruction of Jerusalem in some passages. When Jesus spoke about the coming catastrophe and judgment, He spoke in apocalyptic language. When He indicated that these events would happen during the lifetime of some of His hearers, he was either wrong or He spoke about the fall of Jerusalem in AD 70 (Matt. 24:34). I think He spoke about Jerusalem's fall.

Jesus' Promise

Jesus interpreted the Day of the Lord in the Old Testament as having come to a kind of fulfillment in His own life. He spoke of Himself as the Son of man and of the coming day as the day of the Son of man or the "coming of the Son of man" (Matt. 24:27, 37, 39;

25:31). In the great discourses of Matthew 24—26, Jesus spoke often of this coming. As Matthew recorded, Jesus spoke on the subjects of a coming judgment, vindication and destruction, sufferings, false teachers, suddenness of coming, and preparedness for the event. He responded to questions about the date of the coming events and the signs of His coming (Matt. 24:3).

Even though we are not certain about all of the details, and Jesus did not say when He would come, we are certain that Jesus promised the disciples that He would return in judgment, vindication, and victory. John reported the promise in its most popular form "I go to prepare a place for you . . . . I will come again" (John 14:2-3).

Luke reported the appearance and ascension of Christ along with the promise. The ascended Lord was obscured by a cloud. The disciples stood gazing into the sky. "Two men stood by them in white robes, and said, 'Men of Galilee, why do you stand looking into heaven? This Jesus, who was taken up from you into heaven, will come in the same way as you saw him go into heaven' " (Acts 1:10-11).

The Christian Expectation of Christ's Coming

The New Testament writings frequently speak of the expectation of Christ's coming, attesting not only to the expectation but also to its importance. A brief review of the more important passages will be given.

Paul.—Paul spoke of the resurrection of believers "at his coming" (1 Cor. 15:23) and of his own vindication "before our Lord Jesus at his coming" (1 Thess. 2:19). He prayed for the same vindication of the Thessalonians "at the coming of our Lord Jesus with all his saints" (1 Thess. 3:13). He gave a detailed account of "the coming of the Lord" in 1 Thessalonians 4:15 and concluded the letter with yet another reference to the "coming of our Lord Jesus Christ" (1 Thess. 5:23). He mentioned the coming of the Lord twice in 2 Thessalonians 2:1,8.

Paul also spoke of Christ's return as a "revelation" in several passages. The "revealing of our Lord Jesus Christ" (1 Cor. 1:7) is the same as His coming. Paul expressed the same idea in the words "when the Lord Jesus is revealed from heaven with his mighty angels in flaming fire" (2 Thess. 1:7).

Paul used the word "appearing" synonymously with "coming" in the expression "by his appearing and his coming" (2 Thess. 2:8). The "appearing of our Lord Jesus Christ" (1 Tim. 6:14) is His "appearing" (2 Tim. 4:1,8) and "the appearing of the glory of our great God and Savior Jesus Christ" (Titus 2:13).

Paul spoke of the "day of Christ" or the "day of the Lord" to designate Christ's coming in judgment (1 Cor. 1:8; 5:5; 2 Cor. 1:14; Phil. 1:6, 10; 2:16; 1 Thess. 5:2; 2 Thess. 2:2).

Hebrews.—The Epistle to the Hebrews employs the verb "to appear" in He "will appear a second time" (Heb. 9:28).

James.—James admonished his readers to be patient "until the coming of the Lord" (5:7) and stated, "The coming of the Lord is at hand" (v. 8).

Peter.—The "revelation of Jesus Christ" (1 Pet. 1:7) is the same as His return. In 2 Peter, however, we find the "coming of our Lord Jesus Christ" (1:16), which could refer to His first coming, and "his coming" (3:4) and "the coming of the day of God" (v. 12), which definitely refer to a future coming in judgment.

John.—The First Epistle of John speaks of "his coming" (2:28) and "when he appears" (3:2). The Book of Revelation proclaims, "Behold, he is coming with the clouds, and every eye will see him" (1:7). It concludes with the dramatic consummation of history in the coming of Christ and His eternal kingdom.

The early Christians were convinced that Jesus Christ would come again. That hope was the center of their expectations. Around that hope were clustered other important themes.

Events Related to Christ's Return

The preceding review of the New Testament passages on Christ's return indicate not only the importance of the belief but also something of its scope. In a way, Christ's return is intertwined with several of the major eschatological themes. Their importance is evident in the fact that they appear as chapter headings in this and most other volumes dealing with Christian hope. To avoid repetition, I shall only list these events at this time.

The Lordship of Christ

When Christ returns, "every knee" shall "bow, in heaven and on earth and under the earth, and every tongue confess that Jesus Christ is Lord, to the glory of God the Father" (Phil. 2:10-11). This exaltation of Christ and the acknowledgment of His lordship are also expressed in the the kingdom of God theme.

The Resurrection of the Dead

The coming of Christ will bring to reality this hope for the resurrection as is so eloquently expressed in 1 Thessalonians 4 and 1 Corinthians 15.

The Judgment

When Christ comes again, the final judgment will follow. For the faithful, it will be a vindication, the Day of the Lord. For the unfaithful, it will be a condemnation, a separation.

The Beginning of Eternal Destiny

Following judgment, men and women will go to their eternal destinies.

The Consummation of All Things

In other chapters I write about a new heaven and a new earth, the end of history, and the possibility of a renovated earth. At this point, however, we need to note that the return of Christ means the consummation of all things. It means that God the Creator and Redeemer will bring His Creation to its desired goal. "That all things were to be consummated in Christ was a hope that no Christian could forgo without jettisoning his faith altogether."[4] If one denies this belief, one unwittingly denies the sovereignty of God over the past and the present, as well as the future.

Certainties About Jesus' Coming

The Fact of His Coming[5]

The parables of Jesus about judgment portray human responsibility in terms of a certain accountability. When talents were entrusted to stewards, they knew they would face a day of accounting.

Jesus spoke often about His coming again in judgment and vindication. His promises are adequate for us who believe.

At the time of Jesus' ascension, the angelic messengers assured the disciples that He would come again as they had seen Him leave (Acts 1:11).

The New Testament teachings abound with the expectation of His return. This expectation reflects not only the specific promises but also the logical implication. Since Jesus came in the first place as Son of God and Savior, He can come again to complete His saving act.

The eschatological hope of the early Christians was bound inseparably to their conviction that God had created the world for a purpose. Christ revealed that purpose in His saving work. All of the discussions of this eschatology inevitably come to focus on the coming of Christ (1 Thess. 4:13-18; 1 Cor. 15; Matt. 24—26).

The author of Hebrews placed the coming judgment, the death of Christ and His coming again on the same level of certainty as death. He wrote, "Just as it is appointed for men to die once, . . . Christ . . . will appear a second time" (Heb. 9:27-28).

The Universality of His Coming

The phrase, the universality of His coming, may not be ideal, but it is intended to cover two aspects of Christ's coming: All people will be involved, both the righteous and the wicked; and, His coming will not be in secret. The New Testament writers made clear statements that the coming of Christ will be a *cosmic* event. For the unrighteous, it will bring sudden judgment, as in the parables of Jesus. For the believers it will bring joyful resurrection, which does not omit any believer whether alive or deceased (1 Thess. 4:13-18).

The coming of Christ is also a *visible* event. Some scholars[6] think it necessary to stress the visibility to refute those who would reduce Christ's coming to a spiritual experience or a vision and those who would speak of a secret coming. Biblical discussions mention clearly visible signs, such as the "clouds of heaven" (Matt. 24:30) and that "every eye shall see Him" (Rev. 1:7).

His Coming Will Be Personal

After the resurrection, the Jesus who had died appeared to the disciples. Paul's experience on the road to Damascus may have been a kind of vision (none the less real), but the other appearances were accompanied by details that require us to think of a genuine "bodily" resurrection. Berkhof, guarding against weakening the New Testament evidence, insisted that Jesus' coming will also be physical.[7]

I have previously noted that both body and soul designate the person, hence I am insisting that Christ will return in person. "This Jesus" (Acts 1:11) is the person about whom Paul wrote "the Lord himself will descend" (1 Thess. 4:16). C. H. Dodd, while stating that Christ's coming is primarily related to all humanity, indicated that in a real sense Christ has come for each of us when we die.[8] The coming is still personal.

His Coming Will Be Sudden

Jesus taught us to be prepared for His coming because there would be no time to make even quick preparation. The coming of Christ will be like "the lightning" (Matt. 24:27), as surprising as in "the days of Noah" (v. 37), and as unexpected as "the thief " in the night (v. 43).

His Coming Will Be Triumphant

Christ's coming is pictured in the New Testament as a time of triumph. In contrast to His dying on the cross mocked as the "King of the Jews," Christ will come "on the clouds of heaven with power and great glory" (Matt. 24:30). He will come in glory, and we will share His triumph (Col. 3:4; Titus 2:13). In the Book of Revelation Christ comes as the conquering King who triumphs over sin, death, and the devil and establishes His kingdom forever.

His Coming Will Be Final

Final judgment attends or follows Christ's coming. The clear teaching of Scripture is that today is the day for preparation. It will be too late when He comes. The parables especially stress this finality. The coming of Christ is the opening event of the consummation. Hebrews makes it clear that Christ came the first time to save us from sin. He is our High Priest who made atonement "once for all when he offered up himself" (Heb. 7:27). He will come again, but His mission will be different. "Christ, having been offered once to bear the sins of many, will appear a second time, not to deal with sin but to save those who are eagerly waiting for him" (Heb. 9:28).

Uncertainties About His Coming

We are uncertain about numerous details related to Christ's Parousia. Most often discussed are: (1) the time of His coming and (2) the manner of His coming.

The time of His coming.—Over the centuries the church has harbored those who had little interest in the meaning of Christ's coming but were obsessed with the date for His appearance. They have constructed calendars with all of these future events plotted. Some have been so certain that they persuaded others and together they sold their properties, abandoned their occupations, and traveled to a nearby hill to get the first glimpse of His arrival.

The first disciples asked, "Tell us, when will this be, and what will be the sign of your coming and of the close of the age?" (Matt. 24:3). Jesus answered the question with several illustrations and warnings. His answer should have prevented the question from ever being asked again. "But of that day and hour no one knows, not even the angels of heaven, nor the Son, but the Father only" (v. 36).

After Jesus' resurrection, disciples asked a similar question, "Lord, will you at this time restore the kingdom to Israel?" Jesus responded, "It is not for you to know times or seasons which the Father has fixed by his own authority" (Acts 1:6-7).

The "signs of the times" have been reworked repeatedly by the puzzle solvers in attempts to discover what Jesus Himself did not know. The "signs" which precede the end cannot be identified with certainty. Wars and rumors of wars happen in every generation. Pestilence is common. Some of the statements allegedly referring to the end of the age refer rather to the fall of Jerusalem. Honesty requires the acknowledgment that we do not have the information about the date of Christ's Parousia.

The manner of His coming.—We have more information about the manner of Christ's coming, but it is too little for us to construct a clear picture. Coming with the clouds of heaven, with the trumpet sound, indicate a glorious and victorious coming but leave us with great mystery. Some believe that His coming is individual for each of us at death, while others think of a cataclysmic event at the end of history. We need not know when or how He will come. Knowing that He will come should be enough.

Permanent Importance of the Hope for His Coming

Were the Thessalonians disappointed because Jesus didn't return in their lifetime? He has not come yet in the fullest sense of the word. Does this mean the hope is futile? I think not. It is important, however, that we continue to believe in his coming, be faithful to Him, and live in hope.

A. L. Moore found numerous benefits from this period of waiting in hope.[9] He saw it as a time in which repentance and faith grow and the church grows. It is a time of Christian missions, and an era of the Holy Spirit.

Let us look at a brief summary of ideas which mark the importance of the hope for Christ's coming.

It Moves Us to Preparedness

No theme is clearer in Jesus' teaching about His coming than the necessity for us to be prepared. The expectation of judgment is dreadful only to the unprepared. Christians look forward to Christ's coming as vindication. The expectation of Christ's return motivates us to be ready.

It Makes Our Lives More Human

We are the creatures of God, always dependent upon Him. At the same time, He has entrusted creation into our hands for a short time. We are responsible to Him as we exercise dominion over our part of creation. Creaturely dependence and a sense of responsibility constitute the nature of human existence. We are also creatures of time, with past, present, and future in every moment. This tension describes our freedom.

The expectation of Christ's coming speaks to our human creatureliness and responsibility and directs our tension into creative living.

The Expectation of His Coming Keeps Hope Alive

We cannot live without hope. We must look forward to some future. Christ and His coming place before our eyes a worthy goal toward which we look.

Christ's Coming Endows Life with an Urgency

We are commanded to be alert, watchful, and waiting. Human life must be sensitive and perceptive. Our own preparation for His coming is a matter of urgency. What about our role in sharing this urgency with others? There is no more noble urgency than to live life in the hope of hearing Christ say on that day, "You have been faithful!"

Living Until He Comes

Wherever Christians worship, they celebrate Christ's atoning death through the Lord's Supper by whatever name. The mystery of Christ's presence during His absence continues to endow our worship with reverence. Paul received the tradition and passed it on. He understood

> that the Lord Jesus on the night when he was betrayed took bread, and when he had given thanks, he broke it, and said, "This is my body which is for you. Do this in remembrance of me." In the same way also the cup, after supper, saying, "This cup is the new covenant in my blood. Do this, as often as you drink it, in remembrance of me." For

as often as you eat this bread and drink the cup, you proclaim the Lord's death *until he comes* (1 Cor. 11:23-26, author's italics).

Christian living, like Christian worship, is measured in its breadth, depth, and height by that phrase of hope, "until he comes."

Notes

1. Emil Brunner, *Eternal Hope,* Harold Knight, trans. (Philadelphia: The Westminster Press, 1954), pp. 138-139.

2. For a discussion of the centrality and finality of Jesus Christ for Christians see Morris Ashcraft, "Jesus Christ," *Christian Faith and Beliefs* (Nashville: Broadman Press, 1984), pp. 40-66.

3. John A. T. Robinson, *Jesus and His Coming* (New York and Nashville: Abingdon Press, 1957); Paul S. Minear, *Christian Hope and the Second Coming* (Philadelphia: The Westminster Press, 1954); A. L. Moore, *The Parousia in the New Testament* (Leiden: E. J. Brill, 1966); see also H. K. McArthur, "Parousia," *Interpreter's Dictionary of the Bible* (New York and Nashville: Abingdon Press, 1962), 3:658- 661.

4. Robinson, p. 23.

5. Ray Summers, *The Life Beyond* (Nashville: Broadman Press, 1959), pp. 100 *ff.*

6. L. Berkhof, *The Second Coming of Christ* (Grand Rapids: William B. Eeerdmans Publishing Company, 1953), pp. 40 *ff.*

7. Ibid., p. 36.

8. C. H. Dodd, *The Coming of Christ* (Cambridge: The Cambridge University Press, 1951), p. 31.

9. Moore, pp. 207 *ff.*

6

Hope and the Judgment

For we must all appear before the judgment seat of Christ, so that each one may receive good or evil, according to what he has done in the body (2 Cor. 5:10).

The great baseball player Ted Williams was reported to have said that his goal was to be such an athlete that when he retired his manager would say, "He is the greatest player I ever coached." This wholesome ambition must have been a motivating drive. He was speaking of judgment on the human level. Judgment was not something to be feared; rather, it was a motivating force.

This chapter deals with that kind of judgment on the ultimate level. As you look toward the end, what words would you like to hear God say about your life?

One word will be enough if it is the right word. Jesus told a story about a man who entrusted his wealth to servants while he went on a journey. He gave five talents to one of them, two talents to another, and one talent to the last one. Upon his return, he called his investors in to settle the accounts and to report on their stewardship. The first two had invested wisely and had realized an acceptable gain. The third had feared to take the risk and had hidden the money. The owner said to the first two, "You have been *faithful*" (Matt. 25:14-30, author's italics).

The biblical theme of judgment has been most often misunderstood because people think only of the negative, condemnation. Biblical judgment always offers two verdicts: vindication and condemnation.

A visit to the Internal Revenue Office holds no dread for the person who is honest and keeps good records.

We face many different judgments daily. We go to the physician for an examination and tests, seeking his judgment. We have periodic evaluations in our work. We check the records of our financial holdings and often submit them to accountants or auditors because we recognize the need for judgment, constructive evaluation.

The Certainty of Judgment

Judgment is as certain as death. "Just as it is appointed for men to die once, and after that comes judgment" (Heb. 9:27). The Bible speaks to us consistently and frequently about the certainty of judgment.

Old Testament Teachings

The theme is so common in the old Testament that we will look only at a few illustrations.

In the garden of Eden.—When Adam and Eve sinned against God, they were expelled from the garden. Even before God judged them, however, they had already judged themselves. Whatever they did against God separated them from Him because they had hidden from Him before He came "walking in the garden in the cool of the day" (Gen. 3:8).

The tragic story of their fall indicates that first they distrusted God. The broken trust was a separation. Their guilt was not imposed by an angry or disappointed God. It grew out of their own awareness. Their estrangement was not an exile imposed by another as much as it was a separation, a divorce of their choosing. Even in judgment God continued to love them and made provisions for their safety.

The Tower of Babel.—The building of the tower was not evil in itself. God does not discourage lofty architectural undertakings. The tower builders, in this case, were already estranged from God. They sought to build a stairway to heaven, a monument to their own pride. The judgment of God is close to the consequence for sin (Gen. 11:1-9).

Israel's pilgrimage.—God called the Hebrew people to a special pilgrimage. They repeated a cycle of events: faithfulness, disobedience, judgment, repentance, forgiveness, and a new beginning. The judgment came in various ways, such as national catastrophes. The prophets called them to repentance. This historical cycle indicates not only the certainty of God's judgment but also that judgment is constructive, not destructive. Judgment often leads to repentance and restoration.

The Day of the Lord as national judgment.—The Old Testament prophets spoke of the coming Day of the Lord as a time of judgment. On some occasions, there was hope for vindication and deliverance; on other occasions, the Hebrew prophets proclaimed coming condemnation.

The judgment was upon the nation. Defeat at the hands of an enemy was often understood as the judgment of God. When Israel repented, God forgave and restored the nation.

Individual judgment in Ezekiel and Jeremiah.—In early Hebrew history, the emphasis was upon corporate solidarity rather than individual responsibility. Both Ezekiel and Jeremiah, however, stressed individual responsibility and judgment. They quoted the old adage, "The fathers have eaten sour grapes, and the children's teeth are set on edge" (Jer. 31:29; Ezek. 18:2). That adage blamed one's sins on inheritance. The two prophets continued to stress that each individual was responsible for, liable to judgment, and may die for his own sin.

Judgment in the fall of Jerusalem, 586 BC.—The greatest national calamity up to that time was Jerusalem's fall to Babylon in the early sixth century BC. Before this time God had delivered the nation. Jeremiah prophesied that this time God would not intervene because of the nation's sins. The defeat, destruction, and captivity which followed were understood as the judgment of God.

Jeremiah took no comfort in being right. His lamentation on the fall of Jerusalem is one of the saddest compositions in the Old Testament. He saw the Holy City in the brightness of her noonday brilliance but had to write, "Her sun went down while it was yet day" (Jer. 15:9).

Daniel on universal judgment.—Daniel, without using the word *judgment,* made the clearest statement on general judgment in the Old

Testament. "Many of those who sleep in the dust of the earth shall awake, some to everlasting life, and some to shame and everlasting contempt" (Dan. 12:2).

New Testament Teachings

Jesus on judgment.—Jesus spoke often on judgment. Only a few examples will be cited. Jesus condemned evil and commended true speech by saying, "I tell you, on the day of judgment men will render account for every careless word they utter; for by your words you will be justified, and by your words you will be condemned" (Matt. 12:36-37).

Jesus told several parables to teach judgment. He indicated that people would be condemned or vindicated in the coming judgment on the basis of whether they were prepared, faithful, and responsive to other human beings.

He indicated that people would be surprised in the judgment. He vindicated one group by saying, "for I was hungry and you gave me food, . . . drink" (Matt. 25:35), but they registered astonishment. They had responded to human need and, in the process, had responded to Him. He condemned another group for their failure to respond and they indicated that they had not been aware of their failure (vv. 42-46).

Paul on judgment.—Paul stressed several themes of judgment. In Romans, the "wrath of God" is not the outburst of anger on the part of an offended God. Rather, it is the consequence of sin, a resultant degradation and alienation. Paul argued that people had a natural knowledge of God in their consciences but had worshiped idols instead of God. "Therefore God gave them up in the lusts of their hearts to impurity" (Rom. 1:24). When God continues to call us to repentance and convicts us of sin, we may be uncomfortable, but we have hope in God. When we refuse God so long, we become incapable of response. The result is that we no longer sense even the judgment of God. The alienation is complete. This is the wrath of God.

Paul saw the Jews coming under the judgment and condemnation of God because they had been unfaithful to His covenant with them.

He taught that God judged and condemned the Gentiles because all of them had refused to worship God even though they had a natural knowledge of God in their consciences (Rom. 1:19-20). He taught that we all come under God's judgment "since all have sinned and fall short of the glory of God" (Rom. 3:23), but we can be justified by God's grace (v. 24).

Paul taught that the standard of judgment will be how we respond to the gospel of Christ. "For we shall all stand before the judgment seat of God" (Rom. 14:10). Also, "For we must all appear before the judgment seat of Christ, so that each one may receive good or evil, according to what he has done in the body" (2 Cor. 5:10).

Paul believed in the certainty of judgment. Jesus Christ is the Judge and standard of judgment. One may be either vindicated or condemned; judgment depends on what one did in this life.

Peter on judgment.—Peter's teaching on judgment is consistent with other New Testament teaching (1 Pet. 4:17).

Hebrews on judgment.—We have already noted that judgment is as certain as death (Heb. 9:27). The author also spoke about "eternal judgment" (6:2). In speaking about deliberate sin, he wrote about the "fearful prospect of judgment, and a fury of fire which will consume the adversaries" (10:27).

James on judgment.—James, like the Old Testament prophets, loathed oppression of the poor by the rich. He indicated that the Lord would come (5:7-8) and that He was the "Judge" who was "standing at the doors" (v. 9).

John on judgment.—In the great passage which says "God is love," John encouraged us to live in the love of God because "In this is love perfected with us, that we may have confidence for the day of judgment, because as he is so are we in this world" (1 John 4:17). Judgment is certain, but we do not have to live in dread of it because "perfect love casts out fear" (v. 18).

Revelation on judgment.—The great apocalyptic drama of redemption tells the whole story of sufferings, woes, persecutions, and final judgment. The "great white throne" judgment finalizes all judgment. "I saw the dead, great and small, standing before the throne, and books were opened. Also another book was opened, which is the book of life. And the dead were judged, . . . by what they had done" (20:12).

The Creeds of the Church

A cursory reading of the great creeds and confessions of the church will reveal that they give special attention to the expectation that judgment will come at the close of the age. The old Roman Symbol, a forerunner of the Apostles' Creed, dated about AD 150 included the statement ". . . whence he will come to judge the living and the dead"[1]

The Reasons for Judgment

The overwhelming witness of Scripture is that judgment is a certainty. We may understand the scriptural teachings better if we learn that judgment is very reasonable.

The Nature of Creator and Creature

God as Creator would hardly turn His back upon His creation. Judgment is one way in which God exercises His providential guidance and sustenance. God entrusted His creation to our dominion. Judgment is one aspect of God's supervision over us. Coming under judgment is our way of acknowledging creatureliness.

The Purpose of God

We awkwardly ask, "Why did God create?" The question, asked in this manner, requires us to take a stance before creation which we cannot do even in our imagination. If, however, we work from our knowledge of God's disclosure of Himself in the Bible, we can speak of God's purpose for His creation. We know that God is good and that His creation is good. We know His purpose must also be good. Judgment is God's way of assuring that His purpose will be accomplished. It is reasonable.

The Purpose of Humanity

Many of us grew up having been instructed that the purpose of humanity is to glorify God and enjoy Him forever. If we are God's creatures, we discern our purpose in life in terms of His will for us. *Judgment* is the term which designates the measurement of our faithfulness to that purpose.

Meaning of Responsibility

The nature of human life includes freedom and responsibility. God created us in His own image. That implies freedom and both the ability and obligation to respond. Of all the creatures, we can be alert and reflective; we can sense God's presence and fathom another human being's life. To be in the image of God means that we can respond both to God and to our fellow human beings. This responsibility includes accountability. Accountability is the acknowledgment of the rightness of judgment. We can distinguish between what we are and ought to be. This distinction is judgment, whether God does it or we do it.

The Nature of Human Sin

God created a good world. Sin is a distortion in human life because it marks a separation between human beings and God. It thwarts the purpose of God. It contradicts our role as obedient creatures. Judgment is the act of God which states what is right and points the way for creatures to be right with God again.

Sin is like a disease. It is like a boil on the foot of a child. A foreign element has caused an infection which festers and produces pain and danger. The physician knows that the boil cannot heal until it is lanced and the foreign matter removed. The child dreads the pain of the lancing, but the treatment is the lesser pain and the way to healing.

Our sin against God cries out for judgment. If God did not require it, we would invent it. It is the only way we can be healed. Repentance toward God is painful because it requires that we accept responsibility for our wrong, but it is joyful because it marks the beginning of reconciliation.

Judgment is a logical necessity. It is as old as belief in God. It is inevitable if we are to be related to God because He expects us to move from what we are to what we ought to be. If we are to have the providence of God in history and personal life, we must know that the judgment of God is the constant instruction of God who cares. Judgment is necessary if God is righteous and if human beings are free and responsible.

The Nature of Judgment

The judgment of God is not necessarily a dreadful experience, and it is not delayed until the end of the world. Rather, it is a reality we encounter throughout life. We shall not in any way detract from the idea of a final judgment if we look at the nature of judgment in a broader perspective.

Judgment from the Beginning

Beginning of history.—We have already considered how the judgment of God was first recognized by the parents of the race when they were expelled from the garden. They learned judgment in the negative sense as the result of their sin. In fact, they had already been living under the judgment of God. Judgment is affirmation when we are right.

The belief that God maintains a continuous relationship with His people in their history is the idea of providence. Providence includes guidance and sustenance. God accomplishes His guidance often through judgment. The judgment of God takes the forms of correction, nurture, discipline, encouragement, condemnation, and vindication.

Beginning of responsible life.—Every normal human being at some stage of maturity must accept responsibility for one's life. This acceptance, whether one believes in God or not, is an acceptance of accountability. Accountability presupposes some standard of judgment.

Judgment in the beginning of the Christian life.—The individual begins the Christian life through repentance and faith. Repentance is turning to God from one's sins. Repentance happens when a person hears the Word of God, the gospel, which brings knowledge of the purpose of God and the awareness of one's sinfulness. Repentance includes the acknowledgment of guilt. God's gracious forgiveness is called a "justification by faith." We stand guilty before God in judgment. Through Christ's work for and within us, we go away acquitted, "justified by faith" (Rom. 5:1). Paul argued that we had already been judged and condemned. Now we have been made right with God. Each Christian begins the Christian life in an act of judgment.

All of Life Is Under Judgment

Conscience is a form of judgment.—Paul taught that even people who had not known the law of God had a resident judge within. "They show that what the law requires is written on their hearts, while their conscience also bears witness and their conflicting thoughts accuse or perhaps excuse them on that day when, according to my gospel, God judges the secrets of men by Christ Jesus" (Rom. 2:15-16). This conscience, if developed under God's teaching, is a marvelous form of daily judgment.

Worship includes an element of judgment.—When we hear the Word of God, whether proclaimed, read, or sung, the Spirit of God convicts us of our sins. As we sit in worship, we repent and sense God's forgiveness. Whether we worship in public or in private, we open ourselves to the judgment of God. The saints of the ages have faced their judgment one day at a time; they have rejoiced when God judged, corrected, and restored them to a right relationship with Himself.

Judgment comes in the form of consequences.—Whether we read of Israel in the Old Testament or listen to contemporary Christians, we hear a recurring theme. Our sins bring consequences with them. We sometimes recognize these as the judgment of God. Even though the Scriptures teach and we experience the consequences of sin as the judgment of God, we must be exceedingly careful not to make this interpretation about the lives of others. Jesus condemned such interpretations of judgment (Matt. 7:1). Paul also forbade this passing of judgment on others (Rom. 2:1). Perhaps, we ought to be as kind to ourselves as we are commanded to be toward others. I may be unjust when I condemn myself or interpret some unfavorable event as God's judgment.

Christian life as living under judgment.—In a positive and meaningful way, people refer to all of life as being under the judgment of God. They live each day aware of God's expectations. They measure themselves, or ask God to, by His standards. They begin their days with prayer for God's guidance. They conclude their days with prayerful accounting to God. They accept God's correction as the discipline of a loving parent.

My teacher in Sunday School told us a story which illustrates this theme. In his boyhood, he had known an honored medical doctor who had lived in a frontier region of the country. This physician traveled by horseback in his ministry to the sick. He earned a reputation that was known throughout his region. He was a good and kindly man. The people of the community did not know that the doctor himself suffered from a serious heart ailment which held a threat over each day.

When the doctor was getting old, someone asked him the secret of his useful life. Somewhat embarrassed, he replied by telling about living each day as if it might be the last. After his work of the day, when he returned to his home in the evening, he made notes in his journal. He noted the treatments he had prescribed to his patients so another physician would be able to help his patients. He made his financial records. Then, he read his Bible and prayed. Before retiring, he wrote in his diary. He was facing the judgment every night. Those who looked at the diary after his death noted by each date the same entry, "My house is in order."

Living life under the judgment of God can be a beautiful and meaningful way to live righteously.

The Final Judgment

Beyond individual death, judgment waits (Heb. 9:27). There are several references to the final judgment in the teachings of Jesus and a rather grand picture of the great white throne judgment in Revelation.

Some people would simplify judgment into a single event in which each individual faces God after death. Others believe that the evidence requires a single event in which all the nations of all times will assemble for judgment. The premillennial views require more than one judgment. Ray Summers has listed five such judgments in some schemes,[2] but he does not believe that interpretation is correct. It is more likely that the different references are ways of speaking of the single event.

Some would distinguish between the "judgment seat of Christ" (2 Cor. 5:10) and the "judgment seat of God" (Rom. 14:10), but there is no reason for such a distinction. Ladd has rightly concluded that these two terms are interchangeable and refer to a single event.[3]

The evidence points to a final judgment at the end of the age, but it also points to the practice of judgment throughout life both on individuals and groups. It is certain that those who accept the judgment of God now do not need to live in dread of a final judgment.

The Basis of Judgment

The previous citations of biblical teachings have suggested the grounds on which God will judge us. A brief summary will be adequate.

The Law of God

The law of God summarized basic ideas about God's expectations of His creatures, and on the basis of which He will judge them. Paul, in presenting the gospel of Christ, argued, "All who have sinned without the law will also perish without the law, and all who have sinned under the law will be judged by the law. For it is not the hearers of the law who are righteous before God, but the doers of the law will be justified" (Rom. 2:12-13).

Jesus approved the law as the standard of judgment. To the man seeking eternal life, Jesus said to him, "What is written in the law?" The man summarized the Commandments. Jesus replied, "You have answered right; do this, and you will live" (Luke 10:25-28).

Our Response to Christ

In the same passage in which Paul spoke of judgment on the basis of the law, he spoke of judgment in another way, "On that day when, according to my gospel, God judges the secrets of men by Christ Jesus" (Rom. 2:16). There is no contradiction. Christ fulfilled the law. Faithfulness to Christ certainly equals faithfulness to the law.

John spoke of judgment in the present tense, as if it had already happened on the basis of our response to Christ. "He who believes in him [Christ] is not condemned; he who does not believe is condemned already, because he has not believed in the name of the only Son of God" (John 3:18).

The teaching of Revelation is that final judgment will be solely a matter of the response people made to Jesus Christ.

Judgment and Human Conscience

Judgment is not an outside or alien standard imposed upon human beings. On the contrary, God's judgment is reasonable. Paul's argument about those who have heard the law and those who have not is that all have a knowledge in their consciences which justifies judgment. Obviously Paul did not think the Gentiles lived up to, or passed judgment, on the basis of the "law written in their hearts," but he did insist that this standard of judgment is within us.

Jesus taught people by narrating simple stories which appeal to our common sense. He seemed to think that ordinary unlettered people could understand the simple but profound things of the spirit. He thought we could respond to God and to other persons.

Judgment and Human Opportunity

Eighteen of the parables of Jesus deal with judgment.[4] Whether the judge is God or the returning Christ, the king, the master of the house, or the owner of the vineyard, the idea is clear. The parables deal with preparedness, watchfulness, fruitbearing, and the faithful stewardship of that with which one has been entrusted.

The most obvious thread running through these parables is that judgment is related to our opportunity. Plainly, we will be judged on the basis of what we had. In the parable of the talents, the owner condemned the slothful servant because he had one talent but did not invest it. He commended the others as "faithful" because they managed their trust wisely. Faithfulness designated the behavior of the person who acted rightly in light of the human situation and his or her opportunity.

Jesus' parable of the good Samaritan (Luke 10) indicates that everything depends on the responses we make to other persons we chance to meet. The whole law was fulfilled when one human being responded to another who had been assaulted. He responded to need utilizing the opportunity and resources available.

In the story about the rich man who had everything, including a beggar at his gate, Jesus gave the verdict of final judgment. The man did not go to hell because he was rich or dressed well or fared sumptuously. He went to hell because he did not respond to the poor man who lay starving at his front gate (Luke 16:19-31). Opportunity is an exhibit in the court of judgment.

The Question of Degrees

The question always comes up as to whether there will be degrees of guilt or punishment. Our information is scarce.

Jesus condemned the cities of Chorazin and Bethsaida saying, "If the mighty works done in you had been done in Tyre and Sidon, they would have repented long ago in sackcloth and ashes. But I tell you, it shall be more tolerable on the day of judgment for Tyre and Sidon than for you" (Matt. 11:21-22). He followed that with a condemnation of Capernaum, comparing the city to Sodom.

The passage deals with opportunity and response. It suggests that in the judgment, there will be a difference because of our opportunity. It speaks a message to us but does not really deal with the matter of degrees.

Faithful or Unfaithful?

Reducing the standard of judgment to a single term may be a dangerous oversimplification. But if we do so, there is no better word than the word *faithful.* This word and its opposite take into account our opportunities, limitations, and the expectations of God. God expects us to live in obedience to Him, alert and responsive to other persons. Final judgment may well be summarized in either word *faithful* or *unfaithful.*

The Judge and His Judgment

We shall stand before God, as we do now. Jesus Christ who has made God known to us will be our Advocate and Judge. From Him no secrets are hidden, but He is gracious. He will judge us in grace, as He already has. If we trust in Him, He will sustain us, as He already has.

Before the great white throne will be gathered all people, both great and small. And they shall be judged "by what they had done" (Rev. 20:12).

Notes

1. Paul T. Fuhrmann, *An Introduction to the Great Creeds of the Church* (Philadelphia: The Westminster Press, 1960), p. 26; See also John H. Leith, ed., *Creeds of the Churches* (Atlanta: John Knox Press, 1963), or any other book on the creeds.

2. Ray Summers, *The Life Beyond* (Nashville: Broadman Press, 1959), p. 212.

3. George Eldon Ladd, *The Last Things, an Eschatology for Laymen* (Grand Rapids: William B. Eerdmans Publishing Company, 1978), p. 99.

4. C. Ryder Smith, *The Bible Doctrine of the Hereafter* (London: The Epworth Press, 1958), pp. 149 *ff.*

7

Hope and the Kingdom of God

Now after John was arrested, Jesus came into Galilee, preaching the gospel of God, and saying, "The time is fulfilled, and *the kingdom of God* is at hand; repent, and believe in the gospel" (Mark: 1:14-15, author's italics).

> Pray then like this:
> Our Father who art in heaven,
> Hallowed be thy name.
> *Thy kingdom come,*
> Thy will be done,
> On earth as it is in heaven.
> Give us this day our daily bread;
> And forgive us our debts,
> As we also have forgiven our debtors;
> And lead us not into temptation,
> But deliver us from evil (Matt. 6:9-13, author's italics).

But *seek first his kingdom* and his righteousness, and all these things shall be yours as well (Matt. 6:33, author's italics).

So when they had come together, they asked him, "Lord, will you at this time *restore the kingdom* to Israel?" (Acts 1:6, author's italics).

Then comes the end, when he delivers *the kingdom to God the Father* after destroying every rule and every authority and power (1 Cor. 15:24, author's italics).

And I heard a loud voice in heaven, saying, "Now the salvation and the power and the *kingdom of our God and the authority of his Christ have come*" (Rev. 12:10, author's italics).

The kingdom of God was the central theme in the teaching of Jesus. It is important throughout the New Testament. In the passages cited, note the following. (1) The message of Jesus' preaching was the kingdom of God. (2) The major emphases of the Lord's Prayer place the kingdom of God immediately after the reference to the holiness of God. (3) Jesus taught people to place the kingdom of God first in their lives and let everything else fall into orbit around that nucleus. (4) The early Christians were so obsessed with the kingdom that after Christ's resurrection they asked Him if it were time to restore the kingdom. (5) Paul, when speaking of the end of history, referred to Christ's delivering the kingdom to God the Father. (6) The great victory, dramatically portrayed in Revelation, is complete only when the kingdom of God has been finally established and rivals have been deposed. (7) The parables to which I have already referred often focused on the meaning of the kingdom of God.

A biblical concordance will reflect how frequently the term *kingdom of God* or its equivalent, *kingdom of heaven,* are mentioned. One should not be misled by the observation that the term is not used as frequently in the rest of the New Testament as in the Gospels. These writers knew that the kingdom of God had already begun in the ministry of Jesus.[1]

The idea of the kingdom of God is one of the most important eschatological themes in Christian theology. Many interpreters think that it is not just the central eschatological theme but the only eschatological theme. A contemporary theologian, Otto Weber, stated "The Kingdom of God stands at the center of all Christian expectation and it comprehends everything which must be said about it in detail."[2] The idea of the kingdom of God is the stack pole for Christian eschatology. This term, as much as any other, stresses the constant tension in Christian eschatology between the "now" and the "not yet."

Prophetic or Apocalyptic? Or Both?

In Chapter 1 we considered briefly "Approaches to the Study of Eschatology." Reread that section for the terminology. Some of the eschatological themes of the New Testament are difficult to interpret. Nowhere is interpretation more difficult than in the consideration of the kingdom of God.

The mixture of the prophetic and apocalyptic is one major reason for our difficulty. Space limitations permit only a brief statement. In another volume I have summarized these beliefs and given other sources of information.[3]

Characteristics of Apocalyptic Literature

Apocalyptic literature is a specific literary form which emerged in later Judaism, reached maturity in the second century before Christ, and faded after AD 100. The two greatest works of this type are Daniel in the Old Testament and Revelation in the New Testament.

Apocalyptic literature appeared in times of defeat and persecution, tended to be pessimistic about its contemporary culture, and, though gloomy in outlook at the moment, looked into the distant future for a glorious deliverance. The outlook was dualistic, giving heavy emphasis to Satan, wars in heaven, two ages, and so forth. The literature was deterministic, indicating that in the distant past history had been predetermined and unfolded according to an inevitable plan. Apocalyptic literature featured mystery and secrecy, many visions and angels. It employed animal symbolism using composite animals, strange beasts, and dragons. Often, it stressed numerology, finding or hiding secrets in a series of numbers and dates. This literature featured catastrophic woes and plagues, an abyss and a lake of fire.

Apocalyptic literature is like a foreign language to moderns. To interpret it one must first learn the foreign language. A magnificent collection of intertestamental apocalypses appears in R. H. Charles's edited volume, *The Apocrypha and Pseudepigrapha of the Old Testament.* Reading some of these apocalypses will convince the reader that interpretation is not a matter of "literal" reading. The authors used word pictures to convey truths. The pictures are often exaggerated, told in vivid detail, not intended to be taken literally, as the dragon with seven heads and ten horns of Revelation. John made it clear that the dragon represents Rome which was situated on seven hills and the ten horns were ten kings (Rev. 17:9, 12).

Prophetic and Apocalyptic

Different form.—Prophecy was usually composed of brief, oral, sometimes poetic oracles which were proclaimed. Only later were they committed to writing. Apocalypses were written in the beginning and often were designed in elaborate systems. Revelation, for instance, has seven series of seven visions and interspersed within the book are seven beatitudes.

Reveal or conceal?—The prophets intended to be understood and used symbols to clarify. An example is Jeremiah's vision of the potter's wheel. The apocalyptic writers were intentionally obscure and often declared that their message was sealed until some later disclosure.

Ethical emphasis.—The prophets expressed a profound appreciation for human freedom and ethical decisions which helped determine the future. The apocalyptic writers thought the future had already been determined and were amazingly indifferent toward ethical exhortations.

Views of history.—The prophets were not primarily foretellers of the future. They spoke of the future out of an understanding of the past and present history. They appreciated history. The apocalyptic writers were pessimistic about history. They often took their stance in the remote past under the name of an ancient saint and wrote as if predicting the future.

The greatest difference between the prophetic and apocalyptic writing is this view of history. Apocalyptic writers were not concerned with accurate detailed history. They were concerned about two ages and about great divisions of history which had little, if any, relationship to the calendar.

Mixture of Prophetic-Apocalyptic

In the study of the New Testament statements about eschatology in general, and the kingdom of God in particular, we encounter a mixture of the apocalyptic and prophetic writings. Our concern is to learn the truth indicated. Interpretation is our only method for so doing. It is not an easy task. Often, it means that we have to settle for less than a complete solution to a problem.

An example is the interpretation of the millennium of Revelation 20. John called his book "The Apocalypse of Jesus Christ." If one acknowledges that Revelation is apocalyptic and knows the nature of such literature, then one can interpret the thousand-year reign in terms of a meaning without being constrained to place it on a calendar. On the other hand, if people take the book as prophecy in the sense of history written in advance, the interpretation of the thousand-year reign is quite another matter.

The teachings of Jesus include apocalyptic imagery, such as the clouds of heaven, and prophetic teachings. The disciples often misunderstood Jesus precisely because they were expecting apocalyptic fulfillment of hopes in their own time. Nowhere is this more of a problem than in speaking of the kingdom.

Approach in This Volume

Earlier I noted that Albert Schweitzer believed that Jesus was dominated by the idea of an apocalyptic kingdom to come under His leadership in His time. Schweitzer interpreted Jesus completely from this apocalyptic standpoint in Consistent Eschatology. He thought Jesus was mistaken because the kingdom didn't come that way.

C. H. Dodd, in Realized Eschatology, stressed that all of the eschatological hopes have already been realized in the ministry of Jesus.

John A. T. Robinson spoke of Inaugurated Eschatology as the way. This acknowledges the realized element of Dodd and holds to a future expectation of the prophetic kind.

The Futurist Eschatologies, such as the dispensational view of the Scofield Reference Bible and the popular book by Hal Lindsay, *The*

Late Great Planet Earth, are almost exclusively apocalyptic eschatologies.

My approach is much more rooted in the prophetic than the apocalyptic. I have tried to interpret the apocalyptic in order to understand the eschatological belief or hope expressed therein and to state those beliefs as clearly as I can. I think this approach comes nearer to a true understanding.

The kingdom of God is both a prophetic historical reign of God in history and a future apocalyptic realization. Let us look at the biblical teachings. For additional reading on the prophetic and apocalpytic elements I suggest a book by Georgia Harkness entitled *Understanding the Kingdom of God.*[4]

What the Kingdom Is Not

There are two basic temptations at this point. (1) Some think of the kingdom of God as merely another earthly kingdom with more power than all others. (2) Others think of the kingdom as a kingdom we build for God.

Another Earthly Kingdom

The three temptations of Jesus (Matt. 4; Luke 4) were really temptations because the enticement was something close to Jesus' heart, the kingdom of God. (1) The tempter suggested to a hungry Jesus that He use His divine power to satisfy His personal needs, turn stones into bread. What a sensational way to prove His divinity and gather a following! Jesus wanted no kingdom composed of people who responded for such a reason. (2) The tempter suggested a dramatic exhibition of power by jumping off the Temple tower. That miraculous leap would bring together a following for a kingdom. (3) The tempter showed Jesus the kingdoms of the world and their glory. He suggested to Jesus that He could have them all in one kingdom by accepting the methods of the kingdoms of this world. Jesus refused because He did not want another kingdom like the kingdoms of this world.

John the Baptist in particular and the disciples in general were often confused because Jesus refused to use earthly power to establish a kingdom of this earth. On one occasion John the Baptist even doubted if Jesus were the "coming one" (Matt. 11:2-6). A part of Judas's confusion was the kingdom and power which Jesus refused.

Contemporary churches often forget Jesus' temptations and His view of the kingdom of God. They sometimes compromise with the deceptive methods of the world and confuse numerical success and clever promotion for victory and the work of the Spirit. Some millennialists militantly insist on placing the returning Lord on the throne of an earthly kingdom which He rejected during the incarnation. They would even have Him rule over unbelievers in a kingdom of earthly power and coercion. The kingdom of God, whatever else it may be, is not merely another or greater kingdom of this world.

Not a Kingdom We Build for God

The kingdom of God is not a kingdom we build, even for God. The ancient church, after three centuries of sporadic persecution, misinterpreted its role when the "Christian" emperor Constantine made the Christian church the official church of the Roman Empire. The people believed they had the kingdom of God on earth, but it hardly proved to be so.

Protestantism did not produce a more committed scholar than John Calvin. With his legalistic outlook and his sense of divine calling, Calvin set out to impose his religious rules on the good people of Geneva. He wanted to set up his theocracy, or kingdom of God, on earth. He was too great a man to be selfishly ambitious in his desire to rule the city, but he was not too great to mistake his views for God's views. The kingdom of God was not Geneva, Switzerland, during the sixteenth century. The people lost whatever religious benefit they may have received by their resentment at having their sausages, beer, and games taken away on Sunday evenings.

A number of liberal theologians in America during the nineteenth century and early twentieth century believed we could build the kingdom of God on earth. They named a journal *The Christian Century.* They wrote about "The Kingdom of God in America." The optimistic attitude which nourished this noble dream faded during World War I. It vanished in the atrocities of World War II and in the worldwide violence of the postwar world. The kingdom of God is not something we build at all. Perhaps we may enter it or receive it.

Not a Kingdom God Builds for Us

We are equally wrong when we believe that the kingdom is something God builds for us. The phrase "for us" reverses the direction of the kingdom of God and distorts it beyond recognition. When we speak of the kingdom of God, we must abandon every subtle form of self-centeredness.

Otto Weber pointed out that we have already left the discussion of the kingdom of God when we talk about it in terms of our blessing or immortality. The kingdom of God is not to relieve us of the burden of our world or history. The kingdom of God has to do with God, with God's receiving what is rightly His—lordship, obedience, worship. The kingdom of God is always pointed toward God; it is not something else for us.[5] The kingdom exists, rather, when we happily acknowledge His lordship in and over our lives.

Not a Fulfillment of Our Fantasies

People harbor strange fantasies in their dreams for the future. Hans Küng pointed out a passage in the Koran in which Judaeo-Christian ideas appear in the shadows. There is a description of paradise, sensuously delightful with large-eyed maidens. We make a tragic mistake when we project our fantasies into a future hope for realization in the kingdom of God.

Not a Kingdom Without God

Some childish hopes for the kingdom picture ideals and visions which appear to forget God. Whatever else it may be, the kingdom of God will be what it is because of the presence of God.

The Kingly Rule of God

Definitions

Kingly rule.—Emil Brunner said the Greek phrase translated "kingdom of God" means "the kingly rule of God." "This key-idea of the New Testament means not only the Lordship of God but His Lordship in a humanity unified and bound together by the realization of His will in His kingdom."[6] The definition draws attention to the fact that the New Testament stresses God's lordship and lordship recognized by humanity doing His will.

Redemptive reign.—George Eldon Ladd's view of the kingdom of God is "the redemptive reign of God dynamically active to establish his rule among men, and that this Kingdom, which will appear as an apocalyptic act at the end of the age, has already come."[7] Ladd stressed that this kingdom came in the person and mission of Jesus. Its purpose was to overcome evil and to deliver us from the power of evil. He saw the kingdom as involving two great moments: a "fulfillment within history" and a "consummation at the end of history."

Reign of God.—Anthony A. Hoekema defined the kingdom of God as "the reign of God dynamically active in human history . . . and the final establishment of the new heavens and the new earth."[8] He saw the kingdom as delivering people from sin and demonic powers. He saw the kingdom as including the whole world and that consummation at the end of history. This view includes inaugurated eschatology and a future eschatology.

Guidelines

Reign instead of a realm.—The kingdom of God is the kingly rule of God or the reign of God in the lives of people. It has nothing to do with geography. The kingdom of God exists where God rules and people obey. The most beautiful expression of this purpose of God in the Old Testament is "and you shall be my people, and I will be your God" (Jer. 30:22). It has nothing to do with God's power, which He could use; rather, it speaks of reign in terms of covenant.

This reign is the same as doing the will of God. In the Lord's

Prayer, Jesus taught us to pray, "Thy kingdom come, Thy will be done, On earth as it is in heaven" (Matt. 6:10). The kingdom exists where the will of God is being done; in fact, the two are the same.

Reign as accepted sovereignty.—The qualifying adjective in no way denies or questions the power of God. God created the world, and obviously He has the power to force it and all within it to do His bidding or even to destroy it. God, however, reveals Himself as loving Father and seeks to get His creatures to acknowledge Him, trust Him, love Him as the fulfillment of their purpose. The kingdom of God stresses that realm in which we in faith acknowledge God.

People respond positively and negatively to the sovereignty of God. On the positive side are those who joyfully believe in God and gladly serve Him. On the negative side are those who reject God and come under judgment and separation.

The final vindication of God's sovereignty includes a final judgment. The separation of those who reject God will give a kind of negative acknowledgment of God's sovereignty. That, however, is not the emphasis of the kingdom of God.

God wills not to rule by coercion or sheer force. He created us with freedom and responsibility. He wills that we respond to Him and other persons on the basis of our faith. Life is filled with other persons and challenges, and we live in proportion to our responses. The kingdom of God is composed of those persons who respond in light of their belief in God. If God coerced us, He would destroy us. We would be robots, not human beings.

When people without sensitivity get angry with God because He does not call fire down from heaven, or otherwise correct these evils which abound, they unwittingly confess that they don't want to do God's will but want Him to do their will.

Entrance into the kingdom.—God seeks to bring us into His kingdom through faith in Jesus Christ. The New Testament describes our sinful condition as one of slavery to sin, bondage. When we come through repentance and faith, Christ "has delivered us from the dominion of darkness and transferred us to the kingdom of his beloved son, in whom we have redemption, the forgiveness of sins" (Col. 1:13-14).

A Present Reign

Several New Testament passages suggest that the kingdom of God was present during the ministry of Jesus. Jesus had exorcised demons. He said, "If it is by the finger of God that I cast out demons, then the kingdom of God has come upon you" (Luke 11:20).

Imminence or Presence?

The Greek verb can be translated either way, has come or is at hand. (Compare Matt. 4:17; Mark 1:15.) The same Greek verb appears today on small signs in Greek museums in front of artifacts, in the imperative, meaning "Do not touch!" Even when we translate "at hand," suggesting a future coming, we deal with other passages which stress that the kingdom is present.

The Kingdom Has Come

Similes about seed.—Jesus told several parables which teach the presence of the kingdom of God. Mark preserved one about a seed growing of itself mysteriously and a grain of mustard seed (Mark 4:26-32). The mysterious life in the first seed is just there, like the kingdom, even though we cannot fathom its mystery. The other parable contrasts the smallness of the seed with its enormous potential for growth. The kingdom of God is like this.

Matthew told parables about seed to illustrate the kingdom of God. The parable of the seed sown in four types of soil, while pointing to a future judgment, does so on the basis of what is already present (Matt. 13:3-9). The parable of the weeds also emphasizes a future judgment but answers a question about the reality of evil which coexists now with the kingdom of God (vv. 24-30).

Casting out demons.—When Jesus exorcised a demon from the dumb man, Jesus' critics accused Him of casting out demons in the power of Beelzebub, the prince of demons. Jesus contrasted His kingdom with that of Satan and then stated, "But if it is by the finger of

God that I cast out demons, then the kingdom of God has come upon you" (Luke 11:20).

The Beatitudes.—While the Greek verb tenses are not identical to time in English, it is interesting to note that all of the blessings which will come to the "Blessed" are in the future except the two dealing with the kingdom of God. To the "poor in spirit" (Matt. 5:3) and to those "persecuted for righteousness' sake" (v. 10), Jesus said "theirs is the kingdom of heaven." In one sense, the kingdom already is.

Signs of the Kingdom

The "signs of the kingdom" and the "signs of his coming" again are different. The signs of the kingdom have to do with the evidence that the kingdom is already present. Anthony A. Hoekema listed several signs which point to the fact of the presence of Christ's kingdom: (1) Jesus' casting out the demons, (2) the fall of Satan, (3) Jesus' doing miracles, (4) the preaching of the Gospels, and (5) the forgiveness of sins.[9]

The casting out of demons (Matt. 12:28) and the fall of Satan (Luke 10:18) also point to Jesus' supernatural power. Jesus' response to John the Baptist was in answer to John's question as to whether Jesus was really the Messiah (Matt. 11:2-6). Jesus cited the healing of the deaf and blind, crippled and lepers, the raising of the dead, and the poor have the "good news preached to them" (v. 5). The poor may be understood against the background of Isaiah 61:1. What kind of Messiah Jesus was is related to the kind of kingdom He had brought. His kingdom was already present.

They Called Him Lord

The earliest confession used by the Christians was the simple statement, "Jesus is Lord." This term in the New Testament indicates Christ's lordship. Revelation portrays a persecution of one group of Christians because they would not take the national oath of allegiance which said "Caesar is Lord." They knew only one Lord, Jesus Christ.

The kingdom of God is real today throughout the world. Hosts of men, women, and children begin each day with a prayer to their Lord.

With varying degrees of faithfulness, they live their lives under His lordship. They close each day with a prayer, giving an account of their day and expressing gratitude to their Lord. The kingdom of God is real to them.

A Future Reign

The present kingdom is incomplete. The Lord taught the disciples to pray, "Thy kingdom come, Thy will be done, On earth as it is in heaven" (Matt. 6:10). In a real sense, the kingdom is yet to come. Or, the kingdom in heaven is much more than the kingdom we know now.

The old and new covenants in the Bible depend heavily on God's promises.[10] Abraham responded to a promise of God. The nation of Israel, a kingdom after the days of Saul, lived on a promise of a fulfillment. Jesus Christ in the new covenant was a fulfillment of the hope expressed in the Old (Jer. 31:31-34).

The present kingdom of God in the New Testament looks also to a fulfillment or consummation of the kingdom. It is usually related to the coming again of Christ. Ladd, in a book widely received, has stated that the entire thesis of his book is that the "Kingdom of God was the dynamic rule of God which had invaded history in his own person and mission" and would "manifest itself yet again at the end of the age to bring this same messianic salvation to its consummation."[11]

The End and Meaning of History

The kingdom of God in the future focuses on the ultimate salvation of the individual and the consummation of human history in the kingdom of God. The end of history does not mean its termination. We speak of its goal and completion.

Biblical View of History

The biblical view of history is linear. It begins in creation and moves toward a consummation. Eschatology is not optional in biblical thought. It would be inconceivable to speak of creation in the beginning without speaking of consummation at the end.

Linear history in biblical thought is radically different from the cyclical view characteristic of Greek thought and other cultures. The cyclical view leads toward a repetition and even endless and meaningless cycles of history which have no purpose. In the biblical view, by contrast, history is ever moving from and out of a past toward a future.

Biblical history is not merely human history. Biblical faith depends on God's participation in history. The Old Testament story is the story of God and Israel. Israel's history is a continuum under the providence of God. Naturally, the goal toward which that history moves is of ultimate importance.

The Midpoint of History

Christians understand Jesus Christ as the center of history. Paul stated this as "the fulness of the time" when Christ came (Gal. 4:4, KJV). Previous history was preparatory. God revealed Himself to Abraham, Moses, and the prophets in preparation for His full disclosure in Christ.

Jesus Christ, the fullest revelation of God, stands at the midpoint of history, giving meaning to all which preceded and all which follows. He "is the image of the the invisible God, the first-born of all creation" (Col. 1:15) in whom "all things hold together" (v. 17) in whom "all the fulness of God was pleased to dwell" (Col. 1:19). Jesus "reflects the glory of God and bears the very stamp of his nature, upholding the universe by his word of power" (Heb. 1:3).

Christ, the Lord of History

The pilgrimage of Israel under the providence of God leaves all future humanity in its debt. That unique history became the model of all history. If God delivered Israel from Egypt as the Hebrews were convinced, then God, not Pharaoh, is the Lord of history. History has meaning.

Since Christ is the revelation of God, Jesus Christ is the greatest event in all of history. Jesus' life and work declare for all time that God is at work within history to redeem it. His life inaugurated a new age and pointed to a future eternal age. This is the meaning and direction which leads toward a goal.

The Meaning of History

History is collective human life with purpose. It can never become a monotonous continuity. History has its origin in God and its development under the providence of God; therefore, it is moving toward the goal for which God created it. With Jesus Christ standing at the center, we see the meaning of history.

God's reconciling work illustrates the meaning of history. Reconciliation with God results in reconciliation with others (2 Cor. 5:17-21). Salvation is the same as the reign of God in our lives, the kingdom of God. As individuals, we believe that our lives move toward a distant goal which God approves. Collectively, history also moves toward its appointed end, the kingdom of God.

The meaning of history may be summarized in a number of convictions. (1) We believe that history consists of persons who have genuine freedom who participate in events not totally separated from God. (2) We believe that God is the Creator of the world and Lord of history. (3) We believe that God through His providence has acted within history and continues to do so. (4) We believe that Jesus Christ stands at the midpoint of history, giving meaning to all that preceded and meaning and direction to all that follows. (5) We believe that in Jesus Christ a new age dawned in human history. (6) We believe that history, under the guidance of God, is moving toward a goal in the future. (7) That goal is the consummation of history in the kingdom of God.

The End of the Kingdom of Evil

Biblical faith takes the fact of evil seriously. Evil stands as the most serious adversary to one who believes in God. "If God is good and sovereign, why does He permit evil?" is the question of theodicy. If God is the Creator and if creation is good, whence did evil come?

Evil is irrational, a contradiction. One can hardly give a rational explanation for an irrational act or statement. We cannot explain evil.

We experience it as a devastating mystery contradicting both life and reason. We cannot take the easy way out, dualism, as Zoroastrianism does. We believe that God is one, not two, and that God is good, not good and evil.

Some Christians would elevate Satan, as the Zoroastrians do, to an equal role with God. Others would reduce him only slightly, still having a good god and an evil one as Ahura Mazda and Angra Mainyu of Zoroastrianism. Biblical teachings will not permit it.

The serpent tempted the parents of the race. They listened and disobeyed God. They, however, were responsible for their sin. The devil who tempted Jesus is later equated with the serpent, the dragon, and Satan (Rev. 12:9), but he is not the *cause* of our sin, only the *occasion*. We cause our sin. Satan, however, stands in the Bible reminding us that evil is present, is real, is serious, and is an ultimate threat to us.

Powers and Principalities

The New Testament speaks of evil in many ways. It speaks of the devil, Satan, Beelzebub, prince of the powers of darkness, Antichrists, a dragon, and a beast. It also says a great deal about our own sin and our responsibility for it.

Human life is often pictured as a struggle against these powers of evil. We are admonished to "put on the whole armor of God," so that we "may be able to stand against the wiles of the devil." We "are not contending against flesh and blood, but against the principalities, against the powers, against the world rulers of this present darkness, against the spiritual hosts of wickedness in the heavenly places" (Eph. 6:11-12).

When we understand the universality of evil in our world and the degradation it has wrought in our own lives, we recognize that it is not strange to speak about cosmic powers of evil.

The realm of evil or darkness, however, cannot stand against the kingdom of God. The New Testament portrays Jesus Christ as the victor on our behalf over these evil powers. It is strange, indeed, that He won His victory through His own death. "He disarmed the principalities and powers and made a public example of them, triumphing over them in him" (Col. 2:15). It stands to reason that we should speak of the downfall of these powers when we speak of Christ's victory. It is also reasonable to speak of the fall of the evil kingdom when we speak of the prevailing of the kingdom of God.

Casting Out the Demons

Previously, I said that Jesus' casting out the demons was one sign of the coming of the kingdom. We are not well equipped in the contemporary world to understand all we would like to about the exorcism of demons in the New Testament world. Demonology was a part of the dark world. Jesus had power there. Occasionally the demons were portrayed as recognizing Jesus and yielding to His power. When Jesus comes in His kingdom at the completion of history every manifestation of evil will vanish.

The Fall of Satan

When the seventy disciples returned to Jesus joyfully announcing that the demons yielded to Jesus' name, Jesus was quoted as saying, "I saw Satan fall like lightning from heaven" (Luke 10:18). His vision, or foresight, indicated that Jesus saw the beginning of the kingdom of God.

John, in Revelation, declared in bold apocalyptic imagery that Satan had fallen and was cast into the lake of fire forever (Rev. 20:10). This is the sign that the kingdom of God has come in its fullness.

Ultimate Defeat of Evil

Sin.—Sin is human evil. In the New Testament, sin is an evil power which holds men and women in slavery. Jesus Christ sets us free from the bondage to sin. We have been "set free from sin" and are servants of God (Rom. 6:22).

Death.—Death is the enemy which threatens every moment of life. Death was the ultimate price of our sin (Rom. 6:23). Christ destroyed death for us (1 Cor. 15:54 *ff*).

Satan.—The evil of the world is often seen as personified in the form of the devil or Satan. He is a ruler in the power of darkness. Jesus Christ's redeeming work resulted in the ultimate destruction of the devil (Rev. 20:10).

Victory over sin, death, and the devil.—The ancient Ransom Theory of the atonement maintains that Christ was the ransom which freed us from bondage. For a thousand years it was the clearest way to speak of Christ's redeeming work. Gustav Aulen wrote a marvelous little book to declare this theme entitled *Christus Victor.*[12] He maintained that the entire story of Christ's saving work is a victory over sin, death, and the devil.

John's Revelation presents this victory as the ultimate coming of the kingdom of God. Jesus Christ is the victorious king. Satan who had opposed Christ was vanquished and cast into the lake of fire along with his lieutenants, the beast and the false prophet. Then Death and Hades, personified as enemies, were also thrown into the lake of fire.

The ultimate victory is the consummation of the kingdom of God.

The New Heaven and Earth

If the earth somehow fell under the sway of evil and became "fallen," it stands to reason that the ultimate reign of God will do something to restore the earth.

In New Testament usage, the term *world* has different meanings. On some occasions it means all creation. God so loved this world that He sent His Son to save it (John 3:16). Sometimes it designates human culture which is superimposed upon the created earth. This "world" is evil. Christians are "not of this world" as Christ was "not of this world" (John 17:16). We are very much of this world as creation. We shall understand if we use the word *creation* to designate the world as God created it and think of human culture as the world in its fallenness from God. Then "evil world" makes sense.

The "end" of the world often designates its goal, not its termination. We may, however, speak of the end of the evil world if we mean the termination of the world in its fallenness.

We have numerous reasons for believing that the "end of this world" does not mean the annihilation of God's creation but its renewal or restoration.

The New Creation of Romans 8

When Paul discussed the marvelous work of redemption among and within people, he could not overlook the possibilities for the fallen creation:

> For the creation waits with eager longing for the revealing of the sons of God; for the creation was subjected to futility . . . the creation itself will be set free from its bondage to decay and obtain the glorious liberty of the children of God. We know that the whole creation has been groaning in travail together until now (Rom. 8:19-22).

The commentators have not been able to give us a clear meaning of this passage. It certainly implies that God's redeeming work in Christ goes beyond human redemption to the rest of creation, which also suffered in human sin.

We could speculate. We could couple this with certain Old Testament passages and speak of the restoration of the physical universe. At least, it implies that creation which suffered in our human fall will also share in Christ's redemption. When the reign of God is completely restored it will include a "new heaven and a new earth."

The New Heaven and New Earth of Revelation 21

The new heaven and earth appear to be a restoration or renewal of heaven and earth rather than annihilation and a completely new creation. To suggest that the earth was so corrupted that it had to be totally destroyed may imply that Satan had actually defeated God at this point. A section in 2 Peter appears to do just that. He spoke of the heavens being "dissolved" and the "elements will melt with fire!" (3:12). Then, he indicated that we await the fulfillment of God's promise which will be a "new heaven and a new earth in which righteousness dwells" (v. 13). Even in this apocalyptic language, however, the new heaven and earth appear to come out of the old heaven and earth.

This Is Our Father's World

In spite of the degradation into which we have plunged God's creation, it is still God's creation. It stands to reason that God would not permit us or other evil powers to wrest it from Him or destroy it forever. Therefore, one aspect of the coming reign of God will be the renewal of all creation.[13]

The Millennium—An Interim Kingdom Of God

The word *millennium* is a combination of two Latin words, *mille* which means a thousand, and *annus* which means a year. From *millennium* we get the words *millennial, millennialist,* and *millennialism,* all designating a thousand-year interim reign of Christ on earth. The Greek word for a thousand, *chilia,* is the root word for *chiliasm* and *chiliastic,* designating the same thousand-year reign.

The millennium designates a thousand-year reign of Jesus Christ on the earth in an interim kingdom between this world and the final kingdom in heaven.

The Biblical Basis for a Millennium

All of the biblical references to a millennium appear in a single chapter of the apocalypse of John (Rev. 20). The devil is bound for a thousand years and locked in a subterranean pit. After a thousand years, he is to be released for a short time. During the millennium the martyrs who had been beheaded for their faithful testimony will rule with Christ. After the millennium other dead persons are to be raised, the first resurrection. At the end of the millennium, Satan will be loosed from his underground prison and will again deceive the nations. At some time later, the devil will be arrested again and cast into the lake of fire forever.

There are several references to an interim kingdom in the nonbiblical writings of the period. Many of these writings are preserved in *The Apocrypha and Pseudepigrapha of the Old Testament* edited by R. H. Charles. One of them speaks of a messiah who will reign for a period of 400 years (2 Esdras 5:2 to 7:4). None of these speaks of a thousand-year reign, and other details vary.

The New Testament presents a wide variety of statements about the coming of Christ and the reign of God. It does not, however, speak of a millennium anywhere except Revelation 20. Those who are convinced that the millennium should be placed in the eschatological calendar usually find other passages which can be related to the millennium. One instance is the passage in 1 Corinthians 15:23-28 which speaks of Christ delivering the kingdom to God "after destroying every rule and every authority and power" (v. 24). These interpreters assume the millennial reign precedes this delivering over of the kingdom. Presumably Christ would take control of the kingdom during the thousand-year reign.

Readers who wish to do further reading on millennialism will find sources in abundance. Most Bible dictionaries will have an article on the subject. Ray Summers has discussed the different positions and has given a very helpful chart of the three major positions.[14] The best complete information on the dispensational premillennial position is in the notes in the Scofield Reference Bible. Anthony A. Hoekema has given a thorough and fair treatment in *The Bible and the Future.* One of the better-known books, though somewhat old, is *The Millennium in the Church* by D. H. Kromminga.[15] Loraine Boettner has published a comprehensive volume that is very helpful.[16]

A discussion of the kingdom of God is not complete without reference to the millennial reign.

Most authorities discuss millennialism under three groupings: (1) premillennialism, (2) postmillennialism, and (3) amillennialism. I shall briefly identify the four positions: (1) premillennialism, (2) post-millennialism, (3) amillennialism, and (4) dispensational premillennialism.

Review of Millennial Positions

Premillennialism.—Premillennialists interpret Revelation as a book of history written in advance. The book, as an outline of history, is divided into: (1) the period of the church (Rev. 1—3), (2) the great tribulation (4:1 to 19:21), (3) the millennium (20:1-6), (4) the little time (20:7-15), (5) eternity (21—22).

The interpretation tends to be literal. The millennium is literally a period of a thousand years. The prefix *pre-* on premillennialism means that these Christians believe Christ will return before the thousand-year reign. He will establish His reign on the earth. Some believe Jerusalem will be the capital. Christ will reign over believers and unbelievers until the end of the thousand years at which time final judgment will take place followed by eternal heaven and hell.

Premillennialists think that the gospel will have to spread over the whole earth and that there will be a great tribulation and a great falling away before Christ comes. The great falling away will probably be related to an embodiment of evil known as the Antichrist.

Premillennialists always have a special place in their system for the Jews. This seems to be the result of their dependence upon Old Testament texts to supplement Revelation 20.

Premillennialists believe that during the millennium Christ will reign over believers and unbelievers. This is the most difficult trait of the system. It is quite difficult to think of Christ ruling over the nations who have not believed. We can think only of coercive governmental power. During the incarnation Jesus rejected such a kingdom. He accomplished His reign through His sacrificial death on our behalf.

The brief loosing of Satan at the end of the millennium presents problems to the literal interpretation. Why would God release Satan to deceive the nations again after having him in prison? After this short period of rebellion and war, Satan will be defeated again and consigned to the lake of fire. Final judgment will be followed by the two eternal states.

The greatest strength of the premillennial position is that it can cite Scripture for its schedule. It always makes a literal interpretation if possible. Premillennialists can often refute those who differ with them by quoting Scripture.

The greatest weakness, however, in the premillennial position is precisely at this point. Premillennialists treat Revelation as literal history even though its author spoke of it as an apocalypse. Its visions and images are apocalyptic visions and should be so interpreted.

There are other weaknesses in the position. The entire case is built upon a single passage, Revelation 20, and that in a book of visions. The advocates of premillennialism are hard put to explain why Jesus, who discussed eschatology in Matthew 24—26, and Paul, who discussed eschatology in both Thessalonian Letters and in 1 Corinthians 15, never mentioned any millennium or other interim kingdom. Adherents are also hard pressed to explain why there are two comings of Christ instead of one, two or more resurrections, and as many as five different judgments.[17]

Postmillennialism.—This position is built on the prefix *post-* and means that the advocates think that Christ will return to the earth after the thousand-year reign. The postmillennialists think the present kingdom of God will gradually convert the world during this long period of time. The world will get progressively more godly. The millennium, then, is not a kingdom in which Christ visibly reigns. It is the present reign of God. When Christ returns He will establish His eternal kingdom.

The basic idea is that the gospel converts the world. It gets better until a golden age results. Then, Christ will return to establish the eternal kingdom.

Postmillennialism was more popular during the days of liberal theology at the turn of the twentieth century. The devastating events of this century have destroyed that optimistic or idealistic view of humanity. Two World Wars and other atrocities have left few believing the world is getting better.

Postmillennialism labors under other weaknesses. It has only Revelation 20 as a basis. That passage certainly does not support postmillennialism. The prophets spoke of a golden age, but it requires some coercion to fit those passages with Revelation 20.

Amillennialism.—The prefix *a-* is the Greek letter *alpha* which, when used as a prefix, is the alpha negative. It means the same as the English prefix *non-* or *un-*. The term *amillennial* is an awkward term not entirely acceptable to those who hold to the view, including me.

The amillennialist understands the Book of Revelation to be an apocalypse and, therefore, not to be interpreted as literal history written in advance. Consequently, we interpret Christian eschatology around other events, not a millennial reign on earth. Revelation is a great apocalyptic drama which portrays Christ's ultimate victory over sin, death, and the devil. It is a message of encouragement to Christians who face tribulation and persecution. It promises them victory through suffering, as Christ won His victory through His own cross, not with an army and swords.

The term seems to imply a rejection or a negative attitude. This implication exists only if one has presupposed a literal earthly millennial kingdom. The advocates of this position refuse to make millennialism the center of their expectations. They, too, expect the gospel to be preached to the end of the earth. They see no reason for other preliminary events to precede Christ's return. He has already met all requirements. The second coming of Christ may be viewed in its totality rather than subdivided as in premillennialism.

Amillennialists are criticized because they do not interpret Revelation 20 literally. Others say the position is too general. The simplicity of amillennialism may be its strongest point. Christ may well reign upon this earth. On the other hand, when He returns, the eternal order may begin immediately.

Premillennial dispensationalism.—This specific form of premillennialism appeared during the nineteenth century in the teachings of John Nelson Darby (1800-1882). The view has been popularized in the Scofield Reference Bible.

Dispensationalism interprets the Bible as showing seven great periods of time called dispensations.[18] These are: (1) the period of innocence before the fall, (2) the time of conscience between the fall and the Flood, (3) the period of human government between the Flood and the covenant with Abraham, (4) the age of promise between Abraham and Moses, (5) the period of the law between Moses and Jesus, (6) the period of grace between the ministry of Jesus and the second coming, and, (7) the millennium which begins with the return of Christ and issues in eternity.

The dispensational premillennialists cherish most of the beliefs of other premillennialists but have a much more rigid system. To maintain this position they not only adhere to strict literalism but also include Old Testament passages into their system to support their idea of the millennium of Revelation 20.

They maintain a fundamental distinction between Israel and the church, always reserving a special place for the Jews in the millennial kingdom and in subsequent history.

Dispensational premillennialism labors under all of the burdens of general premillennialism with additional ones. The literalistic approach to Scripture works well in those books and passages intended literally; it distorts Scripture in other cases.

The special place for the Jews in the millennial scheme appears to contradict the clear teaching of the New Testament. The New Testament writers understood the church to be the people of God and the fulfillment of Israel, that the new covenant had fulfilled the old, and that Jesus Christ had broken down that distinction, that "dividing wall of hostility" (Eph. 2:14). One could hardly imagine a clearer statement than, "There is neither Jew nor Greek, there is neither slave nor free, there is neither male nor female; for you are all one in Christ Jesus" (Gal. 3:28).

For a detailed treatment of dispensational premillennialism see Hoekema's presentations of these distinctions.[19]

Concluding Observations

The discussions of millennialism have been very divisive in the church. This is regrettable. Many churches have even written their view into their doctrinal confessions. No ancient creed discussed millennialism.

The kingdom of God is the reign of God in the lives of people now. It will issue in the eternal kingdom of God after the coming of Christ.

The final kingdom of God is inseparably related to God's original creation.

The kingdom of God, which is both present and ultimate, is also individual and corporate. As individuals we acknowledge His reign. Together we are His people.

The kingdom of God gives meaning to life now and hope for what is yet to come. If we have any sensitivity at all, we grieve and struggle with our individual and corporate sins and failures. We participate in the colossal failures of national governments in which greed, hatred, distrust, and self-centeredness corrupt every area of human life. The kingdom of God, in which we hold membership, will ultimately overcome these kingdoms of evil and establish the righteous reign of God. This is our hope.

We grieve for the polluted and corrupted earth, God's good creation. While we cannot understand fully how it will be renovated, we look up in hope when we read Romans 8. The new heaven and new earth are far beyond our horizon, but the Christian believers have just cause to believe they are out there.

As pilgrims, having "been enlightened, . . . [having] tasted the heavenly gift" (Heb. 6:4), we acknowledge the lordship of Jesus Christ and we move on to His kingdom, already acknowledging His reign in our lives.

Notes

1. Emil Brunner, *Eternal Hope,* Harold Knight, trans. (Philadelphia: The Westminster Press, 1954), p. 155.

2. Otto Weber, *Foundations of Dogmatics* Darrell L. Gouder, trans. (Grand Rapids: William B. Eerdmans Publishing Company, 1983), 2:675.

3. Morris Ashcraft, "Revelation," *The Broadman Bible Commentary* (Nashville: Broadman Press, 1972), 12:240-246.

4. Georgia Harkness, *Understanding the Kingdom of God* (New York and Nashville: Abingdon Press, 1974), pp. 17-51.

5. Weber, p. 675.

6. Brunner, p. 158.

7. George Eldon Ladd, *The Presence of the Future* (Grand Rapids: William B. Eerdmans Publishing Company, 1974), p. 218.

8. Anthony A. Hoekema, *The Bible and the Future* (Grand Rapids: William B. Eerdmans Publishing Company, 1979), p. 45.

9. Ibid. p. 46-47f.

10. John Bright, *The Kingdom of God* (New York and Nashville: Abingdon-Cokesbury Press, 1953). See also Rudolf Otto, *The Kingdom of God and the Son of Man* (London: Lutterworth Press, 1938).

11. George Eldon Ladd, *Jesus and the Kingdom* (New York, Evanston, and London: Harper & Row, Publishers, 1964), p. 303.

12. Gustav Aulen, *Christus Victor* (New York: MacMillan & Company, 1951).

13. Hans Küng, "The New Earth and the New Heaven," *Eternal Life?* Edward Quinn, trans. (Garden City: Doubleday & Company, Inc., 1984); Dale Moody, "The New Creation" and "The Holy City," *The Word of Truth* (Grand Rapids: William B. Eerdmans Publishing Company, 1981), pp. 557-594.

14. Ray Summers, *The Life Beyond* (Nashville: Broadman Press, 1959), pp. 209-216.

15. D. H. Dromminga, *The Millennium in the Church* (Grand Rapids: William B. Eerdmans Publishing Company, 1945).

16. Loraine Boettner, *The Millennium* (Philadelphia: The Presbyterian and Reformed Publishing Company, 1958).

17. Summers, p. 212.

18. Boettner, pp. 149 *ff.*

19. Hoekema, pp. 186-193.

8
Hope and Hopelessness

How can I speak about hopelessness? How can I speak about hell? How can I distinguish between them? How can we who have received the grace of God contemplate eternity with God while anyone remains outside? How could we be so presumptuous as to think that we shall spend eternity with God and His people while others are in hell? How can we even speak of hell when we have done so little with our opportunity of sharing heaven with all others?

It is even awkward to include a discussion of hell in a book entitled *The Christian Hope.* Perhaps I should have settled for eschatology as a title, but that would not have solved the dilemma. A certain uneasiness enters the soul when we speak of anyone being lost from God forever.

In the fall of 1946, just after World War II had ended, I enrolled in a seminary class in Christian ethics. A majority of the classmates had recently returned from the war. Some of them had seen human destruction at its worst. We were discussing the ethical issues involved in war. Professor Olin T. Binkley made a statement which some class members would have disputed at first. He said, "General Sherman, during the Civil War, said 'War is hell!' Sherman was wrong. War is not hell. In hell there is no hope."

During these forty years I have often thought of that statement which is the essential difference between hell and all other human suffering. In hell there is no hope.

In all other human experiences we have hope. During the worst illnesses we hope for improvement. During the worst disasters we hope that all will not be lost. Even the drawings on the walls in Auschwitz and Buchenwald reveal traces or glimmers of hope. Even in despair, the opposite of hope, the human spirit finds a small window through which to look with faint hope. When death takes the one nearest and dearest, our souls look beyond to a time when we shall meet again. Those whom I have known who knew they were dying expressed a calm assurance that even in this departure they looked forward to an arrival on the other side. When there is no hope, hell already reigns.

Occasionally we witness the tragic human experience in which discouragement deepens into despondency. Despondency sinks deeper into depression. Depression can go even to the unfathomable depth of despair. But, the nadir is further down. Hell is the absolute bottom from which there is no up, the darkness in which there is no light, the estrangement in which there is no love at all—ever. Hell is the total absence of hope—hopelessness. God tried to prevent it, warned against it, spared no sacrifice to arrest the downward plunge. Hell is the only hole in the whole universe deep enough for people to go beyond the love of God. Hell is hopelessness!

Without Hope but Not Hopeless

In some human experiences, hope diminishes to the point of despair. Hope of some kind is a necessary component of human existence. We are creatures of hope. We look beyond today.

Sometimes we may get a moment of inspiration if we recall what gave us hope. Paul reminded the Gentile Christians of Ephesus that before they heard the gospel they were "alienated from the commonwealth of Israel, and strangers to the covenants of promise, having no hope and without God in the world" (Eph. 2:12). Being without God is the same as being without hope. In this life, however, we are never totally without God and never totally without hope. God cares for us even when we are unmindful of it, even when we rebel and flee from Him.

A Taste of Hopelessness

A foretaste of hell.—There is no such thing as hell in this life because there is always the possibility that people will turn to God. That is a form of hope. The Christian life, however, is often compared to a kind of foretaste of heaven. It appears to follow that the opposite may be true. Perhaps some people in their estrangement from God experience a foretaste of hell even in this life.

We can speak meaningfully of being raised with Christ as a preview of heaven in this life (Col. 3:1). John spoke of eternal life in the present. He said, "This is eternal life, that they know thee the only true God, and Jesus Christ whom thou hast sent" (John 17:3). If eternal life can be known in this life, what about hell?

To live in this world without hope may likewise be referred to as hell in the present, a kind of "realized hell" now. People often use the term, not in slang or profanity, to describe a dark experience in this life. Those who have served long and unjust sentences in prisons sometimes reveal that it was a kind of hell.

Death with no hope.—Death is an experience of dread for most, if not all, human beings. People who know God face death with hope. What would it be like to face death with no expectation of a "beyond" or a certainty that one was not prepared for the beyond?

Judgment without an advocate.—Human accountability is a universal fact in human responsibility. We face judgment every day. Human literature abounds with the idea that at the end of life we face some kind of judgment with some kind of god.

Christians believe that we have an advocate in Jesus Christ (1 John 2:1). We shall not face the judgment alone. We have hope.

Consider how fearful a thing it would be to face judgment completely on your own. Imagine you have been arrested in a foreign country whose language and customs you do not understand. You face trial. An advocate would bring great comfort to you. It would be dreadful to face the judgment without an advocate, without hope.

Questions Often Asked

What about those who have no hope because they never had a chance?—The New Testament clearly teaches that Jesus Christ is the only way of salvation because "there is no other name under heaven given among men by which we must be saved" (Acts 4:12).

In Romans, Paul indicated that people outside the covenant were condemned because they had been unfaithful to the law written in their hearts (Rom. 2:15). We may argue that they could have been saved if they had been faithful. Paul apparently knew of no examples. Paul, however, was not discussing the same question we are.

Salvation is a much broader subject than the matter of final judgment. It means deliverance from sin and self in this life and trust in God. Those who call upon the name of the Lord will be saved (Rom. 10:13), and they can't call upon Him unless they have heard about Him. Faith is a response to hearing the gospel (v. 17).

We also know that Christ gave us a mandate to proclaim the good news to every creature. If we don't do so and they go to hell for not having heard, one could make a strong case for the notion that the wrong crowd is going to hell.

If God in His grace deals kindly with those who never heard, in terms of what they did know, we should not be offended. It may be that we have no right to ask this question in the way that we have. We must proclaim the gospel. We must leave judgment in the hands of God. We have no strong basis for believing that there is hope for those who do not believe in God.

What about infants and others who appear to have no responsibility? —This subject is never discussed in the Bible insofar as I know. It may not belong in this discussion. People, however, ask the question.

The medieval church believed that infants did go to purgatory but were in a subdivision called *Limbus Infantum* which was located near the outer perimeter, away from the fires of hell.

Many Protestants have held to the idea that those who died as infants did go to hell. We have all heard the extreme statements that there are infants in hell not a span long. Usually Protestants who believed infants went to hell did so on the basis of election. John Calvin thought infants went to heaven or hell on the basis of whether they were elect or not. Zwingli, always more liberal and humane than Calvin, taught that children were elect and went to heaven.

Some Protestants make a distinction between "saved" and "safe." They maintain that an infant could not be "saved" because of his or her inability to believe in Jesus Christ, but in some other way is not accountable and is "safe." If this implies that one could not go to hell unless condemned on the basis of his or her own actions in the light of knowledge and accountability, we could assume that all children, mentally handicapped people, and others who are irresponsible would be "safe." The Scripture says nothing on this subject, but many Christians believe it so.[1]

Hopeful Alternatives to Hopelessness

Those who speak or write on the subject of eternal destiny of unbelievers usually focus on three categories: (1) everlasting torment, (2) universal salvation,[2] and (3) annihilation.

Universal Salvation

Universalism, or the idea of universal salvation, states that ultimately all people will be restored to the favor of God. Some believe that there will be opportunities for salvation beyond this life, but, in any event, no one will be finally lost or left in hell.

The idea of universal restoration is not a modernist idea, as many would think. Leaders in the early church advocated the position. Examples are Origen, Clement of Alexandria, and Gregory of Nyssa. In the same general era others believed in everlasting torment such as Tertullian, John Chrysostom, and Augustine.[3]

Advocates of universal salvation build their cases in a variety of ways. They usually include biblical passages and other arguments such as the following.

Biblical suggestions understood as teaching universalism.—Believers in universal salvation quote Matthew 17:11 where Jesus said, "Elijah does come, and he is to restore all things." But Jesus continued, saying, "but I tell you that Elijah has already come, and they did not know him" (17:12). That hardly teaches universalism.

Universalists see the restoration mentioned in Acts 1:6 and 3:21 as a basis for universal salvation.

In his Gospel John cited the statement of Jesus, "and I, when I am lifted up from the earth, will draw all men to myself" (12:32). Drawing "all men" is understood as universal salvation.

Paul wrote, "For God has consigned all men to disobedience, that he may have mercy upon all" (Rom. 11:32). In 1 Timothy we find, "This is good, and it is acceptable in the sight of God our Savior, who desires all men to be saved and to come to the knowledge of the truth" (2:3-4).

This citation is illustrative, not exhaustive. Advocates of the position find universalism in many places, such as in the doxology of Philippians "that at the name of Jesus every knee should bow, in heaven and on earth and under the earth, and every tongue confess that Jesus Christ is Lord, to the glory of God the Father" (2:10-11).

The argument that hell would be a failure for God.—First Timothy 2:3-4 states that God wills the salvation of all. Those who believe in universal salvation allege that if even one person went to hell God would have failed in His purpose. Obviously this argument overlooks any ultimate effects of human freedom and responsibility.

The argument that hell would violate God's goodness and love.— Indeed, God seeks us when we are fleeing from Him. His love is His nature. Could God who loves us so permit one person to be ultimately lost? Would even human beings permit such an unbelievable destiny?

The argument that hell would be disproportionate, unfair.—Even the most righteous persons are imperfect. Even the most wicked have some qualities of goodness. The difference between the righteous and the wicked in this life is not nearly so great as an ultimate distinction between heaven and hell. We can always find unbelievers with high morality and believers who leave much to be desired. The view appears to lean on the idea of salvation by merit or works.

The argument against an ultimate punishment for a finite crime. —Some people argue from ideas of human justice that the punishment ought to be proportionate to the crime. Human sin is finite, limited in many ways. Would it be just to suffer eternally for such temporal offences?

The argument from historical comparisons.—Universalists often cite such historical examples as the concentration camps of World War II as analogies for hell. The whole world now knows of the horrible, unjust suffering of millions whose only offense was that of being born to Jewish parents. The starvation, hard-work annihilation of six million Jews (and millions more died in other crimes during the period) confined to camps stands as a historical picture of hell.

Universalists ask, Could God and the righteous enjoy heaven knowing that over some horizon in some pit there was such a concentration camp lasting for all eternity? If hell were a concentration camp and if God sent people there, the argument would be hard to refute. If, however, people insist on going to hell over God's objections, it is a different matter.

Universalists finally rest their case on the unsearchable love of God and the ultimate triumph of that love for all persons.

Annihilation or Conditional Immortality

Those who cannot accept the reality of everlasting hell and are unconvinced about universal salvation, have another alternative: eternity with God for the righteous and annihilation for the wicked.

Annihilation focuses on the idea that at some point those who reject salvation just cease to be. This is not some kind of horrible death. Advocates of this view vary. Some believe that the wicked will just not be resurrected, but will cease to be. Others believe there will be a limited period of punishment since sin does deserve punishment.

The arguments are similar to those for universalism. Would the God of love permit or will eternal punishment? Since God's judgment is otherwise redemptive, how would hell be redemptive? Eternal hell would permit the continuance of evil as long as God and good endure. Would that be right? Advocates of hell see the notion as a deterrent to sin. Advocates of annihilation argue that the threat of ceasing to be would be an adequate deterrent if such deterrents work anyway.

Biblical passages supporting conditional immortality are hard to locate. Paul wrote about the "enemies of the cross of Christ" that "their end is destruction" (Phil. 3:18-19), but does destruction mean annihilation? The psalmist wrote, "The Lord preserves all who love him; but all the wicked he will destroy" (Ps. 145:20). It is unlikely that the psalmist and Paul thought either of eternal life or eternal destruction.

Several biblical passages refer to "perishing" (1 Cor 1:18; 2 Cor. 2:15; 4:3). It is alleged that these cease to be. The same word is used of the righteous in Isaiah (57:1).

The figure of fire often appears in the fate of the wicked. Fire destroys, so it is argued that this supports annihilation. Fire also purges. The Holy Spirit is described by the term *fire* (Luke 3:16; Acts 2:3), not meaning destruction at all.

The biblical evidence is not convincing for this position. The most serious argument by far is found in the questions, Why would God raise the wicked from the dead to condemn them to an everlasting torment when all of His other judgments are redemptive in nature? If there is no hope of redemption, is there any justification for punishment? And if so, why forever?

Other Alternatives

We shall look at two other suggestions for the destiny of the wicked.

Degrees of suffering.—I previously noted the suggestion that there may be degrees of guilt in judgment. Jesus' statements to the cities of Galilee that it would be "more tolerable" for Sodom and Gomorrah and for Tyre and Sidon in the day of judgment because those ancient cities had not heard the gospel. On this basis it is inferred that hell will feature differing degrees of punishment.

Purgatory.—The Roman Catholic Church has taught that there is a place of temporary punishment beyond death from which people may be moved to eternal life with God. Those who died in faith but still guilty of venial sins will, theoretically, undergo a temporary punishment and cleansing.

No biblical evidence supports this idea. Advocates appeal to 2

Maccabees (12:39-45), an Apocryphal book. Some cite an incidental statement of Jesus. While speaking about the sin against the Holy Spirit, Jesus said, "Whoever says a word against the Son of man will be forgiven; but whoever speaks against the Holy Spirit will not be forgiven, either in this age or in the age to come" (Matt. 12:32). Does this imply that there will be an opportunity for forgiveness "in the age to come"? The customary interpretation of this passage—that persons guilty of this sin would never be forgiven—has nothing to do with purgatory. Protestants, in general, have found nothing convincing about the idea of purgatory.

The views summarized here express the genuine hopes of many people. They do take God's love seriously. They enjoy logical support. They have a large following. They all face one major difficulty, however. The biblical evidence rather clearly focuses on a twofold destiny for human beings: everlasting life with God or everlasting estrangement from God.

Everlasting Hopelessness

Biblical Teachings About Hell

Old Testament ideas.—The Old Testament, in the early period, concerned itself with the destiny of the nation, not the individual. Sheol was the place of the dead. It was certainly not heaven, but it was not hell either. It was a gloomy realm separate, shadowy, and undesirable.

The only Old Testament passage which seems to reflect an everlasting hell, such as we meet in the New Testament, is Daniel 12:2: "Many of those who sleep in the dust of the earth shall awake, some to everlasting life, and some to everlasting contempt."

The period between the Testaments witnessed the growth of the idea of hell, as the writings of the time indicate.

New Testament ideas.—Jesus said a great deal about hell. If the Gospels did not include these teachings, we might interpret hell in Revelation as an apocalyptic image meaning something other than everlasting estrangement from God. Those who believe in Jesus

Christ, however, and hold to a high view of Scripture, do not have that option. Jesus said too much about hell for us to avoid it.

In the Sermon on the Mount, Jesus stressed the seriousness of our mistreatment of other persons. "But I say to you . . . whoever says, 'You fool!' shall be liable to the hell of fire" (Matt. 5:22). In the same chapter, He said that if our eye causes us to sin or if our right hand causes us to sin it would be better to remove those two members of the body than to be "thrown into hell" (vv. 29-30). While encouraging His followers to be fruitful, He reminded them that "every tree that does not bear good fruit is cut down and thrown into the fire" (7:19). He told them not to fear the people who could kill them but, rather, to "fear him who could destroy both soul and body in hell" (10:28).

Luke's account of the rich man and Lazarus portrayed Hades rather than hell, but the rich man was "in anguish in this flame" (16:24). The great chasm between the two prevented any going back and forth. The state of the rich man was hopeless.

John reported Jesus' teaching about the true vine. Jesus said, "If a man does not abide in me, he is cast forth as a branch and withers; and the branches are gathered, and thrown into the fire and burned" (John 15:6).

New Testament Pictures of Hell

The New Testament gives a number of pictures or illustrations of hell. Let us look at several of those which give a clear insight into the belief in everlasting separation from God.

Gehenna.—The Greek word translated *hell* is the word *Gehenna.* Gehenna was the Greek name for the valley of Hinnom located in a ravine south of Jerusalem. Hinnom, or Gehenna, was the city dump during the New Testament era. Into this dump the inhabitants threw the refuse of the city—garbage, dead animals, and occasionally human corpses. Earlier in the days of the Hebrew monarchy, it had been the scene of idolatrous worship, sacrificing of children (2 Kings 23:10; Jer. 7:31).

City dumps are not common today in this country. When I was a boy, I frequently passed the city dump near the town in which I grew up. The trucks dumped the refuse which included cans, bottles, trash, broken furniture, and appliances. Rats infested the dump because garbage was there too. The combustible materials deeply in the dump burned incessantly. Even the heavy rains did not sink deep enough to quench the simmering or stop the smoking. Gehenna was like that. Gehenna was the New Testament symbol for hell.

When the New Testament speaks of people going to hell, it implies waste, loss, rejection.

Waste and loss.—God created people in His own image, gave them freedom, responsibility, and a world full of challenge. Whatever else we may say about our lives in this world, we must speak of meaning in terms of relationship to God and His purpose and our meaningful involvement with other persons. Our destiny is with God and His people. We are like building stones in God's temple (Eph. 2:19-22). We are like leaves and branches related to the true vine (John 15). We are like members of God's family (Eph. 2:19).

Hell is the state or place of those who chose not to respond to God or to live according to his purpose.

Hell is the place of waste and loss, where unused stones are cast, where unfruitful branches waste, where people go who would not be members of the family.

When a child is lost in the forest, city, or on a river, whole communities lay aside their work and search for the lost. Children are not supposed to be lost. When lost they are in danger. What a tragic loss when a person is lost permanently. When an airliner crashes, we cringe at the loss of life. The whole world grieves when a ship is lost or a submarine sinks or an earthquake devastates a city or a volcano destroys a community. Our minds go to those who died, to the grieving bereaved. Hell is an ultimate loss.

Ultimate waste and loss.—For many reasons or for no reason at all people refuse God, reject human destiny, choose lives without purpose, and proceed to ultimate loss.

The lake of fire.—The smoke ascended from Gehenna night and day, summer and winter. Hell is pictured as a lake of fire. Fire may be the symbol of cleansing or the presence of the Holy Spirit, but it may also be the symbol of destruction.

The unfruitful branches were thrown into the fire. Revelation speaks of a lake of fire (Rev. 19:20; 20:10, 14-15; 21:8) into which the beast and false prophet were "thrown alive." Then, "the devil who had deceived them was thrown into the lake of fire and brimstone where the beast and false prophet were, and they will be tormented day and night for ever and ever" (Rev. 20:10). "Then Death and Hades were thrown into the lake of fire. This is the second death, the lake of fire" (v. 14).

All people whose names were not "found written in the book of life" were "thrown into the lake of fire" (v. 15). In the final judgment, the "cowardly, the faithless, the polluted, . . . murderers, fornicators, sorcerers, idolaters, and all liars, . . . the lake that burns with fire and sulphur, which is the second death" (Rev. 21:8).

This apocalyptic picture of hell as a lake of fire has been the dominant idea of hell and has inspired both literature and painting. If taken literally, it raises many questions we cannot answer. If taken as an apocalyptic picture of eternity without God, it presents a horrible prospect without any hope—utter hopelessness.

Outer darkness.—On at least three occasions Jesus spoke of the condemned as being cast into outer darkness (Matt. 8:12; 22:13; 25: 30). In all three instances there are references to "weeping and gnashing of teeth" (KJV). The symbol of outer darkness is quite incompatible with the lake of fire. This picture must be understood by contrast. The presence of God is often described in terms of light. Christians are the light of the world. God is light and brings light into the lives of His creatures. Hell is the opposite.

Estrangement.—Hell is the place of eternal separation from God. Adam and Eve were expelled from the garden of Eden. Human life is in fellowship with God and community with other persons. Exclusion is the result of human sin. Alienation and estrangement replace community. The most severe condemnation by Jesus was worded, "Depart from me, you cursed, into the eternal fire prepared for the devil and his angels" (Matt. 25:41).

Hell is the final separation from God and human community.

Consciousness and memory.—The human characteristic of holding the past, present, and future in every moment of consciousness extends into eternity. A human being deprived of these abilities is subhuman. We have previously noted the importance of memory, awareness, and hope.

Hell appears to be that eternal destiny for those who have been separated from God but are fully conscious. Their memory and awareness remain unchanged; their anticipation about the future, however, is diminished from hope to hopelessness.

Everlasting duration.—The attempt to shorten hell by the view of annihilation proved unsuccessful. The word *everlasting* designates a continuation without end. The same word designates the duration of the destiny of the righteous. I know of no legitimate way to speak of hell in less than everlasting time.

The second death.—Since death is end or termination, some see the second death as annihilation. The author of Revelation (20:14; 21:8) specified that in the lake of fire "they will be tormented day and night for ever and ever" (20:10).

If life is more than biological functioning, and it is, then death is more than cessation. Death is the opposite of all that life is. It is separation, not extinction.

Ultimate absurdity.—Most people have a sense of meaningfulness in life. They see a reason for living. In the 1950s a strange phenomenon appeared in literature and art—the theme of the absurd. Some of these thinkers had concluded after the senseless slaughter of the twentieth century, life had no meaning, no purpose. Examples are Jean Paul Sartre's *No Exit* and Albert Camus's *The Plague* and *The Fall.* There is a sense in which the authors betrayed their theme by expressing meaning even in writing about its absence.

If one can imagine a life without values, goals, hopes, friendships, obligations, and nothing worth time and thought, that person may sense the theme of meaninglessness.

Belief in God gives meaning to life. If we are the creatures of God, we have a destiny, a purpose. Our purpose is intricately bound up with other persons. We serve God through our relationships with others.

Human sin is an attempt to go it alone, without God and others. The parents of the race decided they could do better without God. They listened to the tempter. Isaiah described this self-centered tendency of sin as "we have turned every one to his own way" (Isa. 53:6). Jesus sought to reverse the human sinful direction when He said, "If any man would come after me, let him deny himself and take up his cross and follow me" (Matt 16:24). To deny oneself has nothing to do with eating or not eating; rather it has to do with who is master of one's life.

Human beings in sin move away from God into self-centeredness. Meaning deteriorates away from God and others. We lose the reason for being. Hell is ultimate meaninglessness. It has no God, no companion to love, nothing to live for or toward. It is ultimate absurdity.

Conclusion

Speaking about hell brings no joy. There will be no satisfaction in being "right" about it. In speaking about hell, the Christian experiences a deep uneasiness. It is so contrary to the entire Spirit of God and people.

The evidence of the Bible strongly supports the teaching of hell as the final destiny of those who reject God. All attempts to evade the teaching or reduce it to something else leave us unconvinced.

The theology of Christians, based upon God's revelation in Christ as narrated in the Bible, understands human beings as creatures of God, both free and responsible. All affirmations of universal salvation ultimately say that we are not really free. If we say *no* to God only to have that *no* changed in some later life to *yes*, it was not *no* in the first place. It was really *not yet*. If all our noes to God are really not yets, and all our not yets are destined eventually to become yeses, we are puppets, not men and women, even though the string may be indefinitely long.

As human beings we have the glorious privilege of saying yes to God and enjoying Him forever. We also have the frightful freedom of saying no to God, now and forever. God does not coerce us. God calls us. Salvation is by faith in Jesus Christ. You and I cast the deciding vote on whether or not we will trust God. Some choose a destiny—here and hereafter—without God.

Notes

1. Harry Buis, *The Doctrine of Eternal Punishment* (Philadelphia: The Presbyterian and Reformed Publishing Company, 1956), p. 140.

2. Ibid., p. 104; John Sutherland Bonnell, *Heaven and Hell, a Present-Day Christian Interpretation* (New York and Nashville: Abingdon Press, 1957).

3. Donald G. Bloesch, *Essentials of Evangelical Theology* (San Francisco: Harper & Row, Publishers, 1978), 2:214.

9

Hope and Eternal Life

For God so loved the world that he gave his only Son, that whoever believes in him should not perish but have eternal life (John 3:16).

And this is eternal life, that they know thee the only true God, and Jesus Christ whom thou hast sent (John 17:3).

For the wages of sin is death, but the free gift of God is eternal life in Christ Jesus our Lord (Rom. 6:23).

Then I saw a new heaven (Rev. 21:1).

We have come to the last theme in our Christian hope—everlasting life with God. The popular term is *heaven*. In the Bible, the word *heaven* usually designates the upper sphere, or upper half, of creation, the sky. As such, it was the dwelling place of God.

The word *heaven* appears 284 times in the New Testament. As the dwelling place of God, it can even be used as a synonym for the kingdom of God or the kingdom of heaven. They are the same. The New Testament often speaks of heaven and earth together, the two halves of creation. Heaven is God's creation as is the earth. When the earth passes away, so does heaven (Mark 13:31). God is Lord of heaven and earth (Matt. 11:25). The saving work of Jesus Christ includes heaven as well as earth "to unite all things in him, things in heaven and things on earth" (Eph. 1:10).

Therefore, Christians naturally think of going to heaven. Jesus came down from heaven and ascended back to heaven. The early creeds usually closed with a statement of belief in "everlasting life" or "the life everlasting." I have chosen to focus on the terms *eternal* and *everlasting life.*

By using the term *eternal life,* I wish to stress first of all that we will be with God. We Christians have frequently been accused of being "other worldly," with some justification. Our accusers have said we are more concerned with the next world than this one. The accusation grew out of resentment that we were not very good citizens of this world. Some Christians have concluded that the world is wicked and going to hell so they have tried to abandon it.

Biblical faith unites heaven and earth. Both belong to God. Both must respond to God's creative work in bringing all creation to its consummation.

The continuity between earth and heaven is obvious in the biblical teachings about our hope of eternal life with God. Heaven, or eternal life, will be the consummation of God's creation.

Eternal Life as Consummation

Completion of Human Creation

God created heaven and earth. God created human beings with a special characteristic—"the image of God." This phrase designates our basic nature. We were created for a special relationship with God and each other. We can respond. Being capable of understanding and reflection, we can reach beyond ourselves and enter into fellowship with God and other persons. God can reach out to us, and we can hear and respond.

Responsibility in freedom is our nature, our destiny. We were placed on the earth with dominion over it. Our destiny was to live "under God," "above nature," and "with other persons." This in-between kind of existence is one of tension. Out of that tension, knowing God's infiniteness and our finiteness, we sinned.

Our sin remains a mystery. The tragic narrative of Genesis 3 is the story of every one of us. We turned away from God, despoiled His creation, and turned against one another. In spite of this irresponsible behavior, we are still responsible. We are guilty. We confess that we live lives on a plane lower than it should be and for goals that are unworthy. We are responsible in that we do respond to God in repentance and faith. Eternal life is the hope that we shall return completely to the destiny for which God created us.

The whole biblical record speaks of God's work for human redemption and our responses, both the good and the bad. We were estranged from God, but God sought to redeem us, restore us. The belief in eternal life is the belief in the completion of our redemption.

Consummation of Redemption

Salvation may be viewed as an event completed when we believe in Christ. John called it a new birth (John 3:3). Paul spoke of a new creation (2 Cor. 5:17; Gal. 6:15). Salvation may also be discussed in terms of the future, its completion. Paul wrote, "Salvation is nearer to us now than when we first believed" (Rom. 13:11). Peter completed his summary of the faith by saying, "As the outcome of your faith you obtain the salvation of your souls" (1 Pet. 1:9).

Eternal life, then, is properly thought of as the consummation of our redemption. It means that God's redemptive work will come to a desirable completion in the eternal presence with God.

Consummation of Creation

We usually think of the Genesis account of creation as implying that God created everything that ever was to be. This leads to a static view of creation. God's work in history, in providence, and New Testament ideas about a new creation suggest that God the Creator has not been idle since the creation in Genesis.

The vision of the consummation speaks of a new heaven and a new earth. Perhaps, we should think of eternal life with God as the consummation of the good creation which God inaugurated in Genesis. We are undergoing a new creation in the discipline of the Christian life. In heaven we shall be the creatures God intended us to be.

The Meaning of Human Destiny

At times we have lost our way because we lost our bearings. We lost those navigational markers by which we maintain our orientation and our course. Despite the confusion and the bewildering ills which have attended our individual lives and our lives together, our hope will not die. We have a deep-seated conviction that life has meaning, purpose.

The deep conviction, encouraged by the promises of God in the Bible, and nourished by the lives of others with hope, moves us to look into the future with hope. This belief in purpose is best understood from the standpoint of God's purpose for us in creation. Then, our human longing is to realize our destiny which is none other than the purpose of God for us. Whatever else we may think or say about everlasting life, we must insist that it is that ultimate destiny for which God created us.

Consummation, the Kingdom of God

I stated in a previous chapter that the kingdom of God is the reign of God in the lives of those who believe in Him. This kingdom is both present and future. When the kingdom comes in its fullness, the will of God will be done on earth and in heaven.

Eternal life, then, is the fulfillment of the kingdom of God. This terminology keeps the focus on God where it belongs. If we think of heaven from any other standpoint, we tend to think of it as a place where we go when we die or a place in which we will be rewarded. Too much emphasis on rewards leads to a self-centeredness and an emphasis on merit. Baron Von Hügel wrote early in this century about eternal life, "Yet it is not man or men, but God Who, here as everywhere in Jesus' experience and teaching, is the beginning, centre, medium, and end of the whole of this final life."[1]

In the culture of the late twentieth century, we think of life as the things we get and have. Seeing eternal life as the consummation of God's kingdom is a much-needed corrective. Heaven is not something else we get to add to our collection, which has resulted from inordinate greed. Rather, heaven is God's kingly rule finally accepted joyfully by God's creatures.

Eternal life will be faithful and joyful existence under the reign of God, just as the Christian life is the same thing in this life.

Consummation of Human Hope

The human spirit will not long languish in despair. Deep within us is an upward look. I believe that is evidence of God's image within us.

Hope, promises, and purpose.—Those of us who believe in God live our daily lives with buoyancy born of God's promises. We are witnesses, as was Abraham, that God keeps His promises. We believe that God has called us to serve Him and promised us His presence here and hereafter. The resulting hope in our lives is a major motivation. Heaven, although it must be much more, will be the realization of those genuine expectations born of hope engendered by the promises of God.

Before His departure, Jesus promised our forebears in the faith, "When I go and prepare a place for you, I will come again and will take you to myself, that where I am you may be also" (John 14:3). We live this life expecting the fulfillment of that promise.

Ultimate affirmation of hope.—Eternal life will be more than a fulfillment of a promise. It is more than future vindication. It is an affirmation that hope is the basic character of human existence. The writers of the New Testament, inspired as they were, saw this mystery. Paul wrote, "we are justified by faith," and have "peace with God through our Lord Jesus Christ." We stand "in grace . . . We rejoice in our hope of sharing the glory of God." But sufferings are real and dangerous. With hope, however, "we rejoice in our sufferings, knowing that suffering produces endurance, and endurance produces character, and character produces hope, and hope does not disappoint us" (Rom. 5:1-5). Eternal life affirms hope as the human norm for everyday living.

Final reconciliation.—*Reconciliation* is the beautiful New Testament word which describes God's work of salvation for and within us. Since Cain and Abel, we have been estranged not only from God but also from one another. As Christians we yearn for that harmony with others which we do not yet have. We long for that reconciliation with God which we know only in part. We long for relief from doubt, anxiety, and division of loyalty. In the life everlasting we shall know the final reconciliation with God and with those other persons with whom we live in estrangement.

Similes About Eternal Life

We shall conclude our discussion of Christian hope, in general, and belief in eternal life, in particular, by looking at some of those New Testament terms and ideas with which eternal life is compared.

Heaven Is Like Home

Those of us who grew up in happy homes with both parents and siblings have an advantage over those who did not know such homes. We, however, run a risk. We may sentimentalize heaven in terms of our earthly homes. Some of the gospel songwriters have done so; but even in their emotional excess, they have said something worthwhile about our hope for an eternal home with God.

People who are required to live long periods away from home can grasp this idea easily. A chaplain who served in the Pacific with the Forty-first Division told a story which illustrated this idea well. He had lived in great danger for many months. He received word from home only rarely. He had seen his friends killed. When his turn came to return to the States, even though the seas were still patrolled by hostile submarines, he looked forward with a renewed joy in life. Each day, despite the surrounding dangers, his hope increased. He spoke of the first inspiring glimpse of the Golden Gate Bridge. His mind leaped beyond to home, family, love, and safety. He said that he always thought of heaven in terms of that vision. Heaven is home.

Jesus said, "In my Father's house . . . I will come again and will take you to myself, that where I am you may be also" (John 14:2-3). Heaven will be a home in which we enjoy blessed fellowship, a place in which we live with God and others, with rest, love, understanding, and permanence.[2]

Heaven Is Like a City

The Hebrews learned from their journey to Canaan, the wilderness wandering, and the Exile that life is like a pilgrimage. Abraham, for instance sojourned in a Land of Promise, moving toward a habitation of God's promise. The writer of the Book of Hebrews said of Abraham, "For he looked forward to the city which has foundations, whose builder and maker is God" (11:10). The earthly city Jerusalem became the city of God on earth and the symbol of the heavenly city (12:22).

In dramatic imagery, John concluded his Apocalypse victoriously with a vision of the "holy city, new Jerusalem, coming down out of heaven from God, prepared as a bride adorned for her husband" (Rev. 21:2). John continued to speak of God being with His people. His statement includes the Old Testament hope that "God will be their God and they shall be his people." John wrote, "He will dwell with them, and they shall be his people, and God himself will be with them; he will wipe away every tear from their eyes, and death shall be no more, neither shall there be mourning nor crying nor pain any more" (Rev. 21:3-4).

Heaven, then, is like a city, the New Jerusalem, the city of God. It is the place of our eternal dwelling with God. This simile of the city has often been a helpful insight into the nature of heaven. Ryder Smith spoke of the geographical account of the future kingdom as being summed up this way: "It includes the universe, and it centers in a city."[3]

Ray Summers, on the basis of a detailed discussion of the passage in Revelation 21:9-17, interpreted the symbolism of the city with special emphasis on its beauty. He thought John had emphasized that heaven is a perfect city, perfect in purity, beauty, and security.[4]

Dale Moody also paid special attention to "The Holy City"[5] as our best description of heaven.

Heaven Is Like an Inheritance

Peter's summary of Christian beliefs reads, "By his great mercy we have been born anew to a living hope through the resurrection of Jesus Christ from the dead, and to a inheritance which is imperishable, undefiled, and unfading, kept in heaven for you" (1 Pet. 1:3-4).

Numerous passages speak of heaven as an inheritance and about inheriting the kingdom (1 Cor. 6:9; Matt. 5:5; 19:29; Mark 10:17; 1 Cor. 15:50; Gal. 4:30). This particular simile not only inspires us to hope for the inheritance; it also reminds us that heaven is the gift of God to us, not something we are entitled to. This figure of speech introduces an element of joy and gratitude.

Heaven Is Like a Garden

The human story begins in a garden, the garden of Eden. It reaches its final consummation in a garden. In the last chapter of the Bible, we come again to the "river of the water of life," the "tree of life with its twelve kinds of fruit, yielding its fruit each month; and the leaves of the tree were for the healing of the nations." There will be no curse in this garden (Rev. 22:1-3).

The river, trees, and fruit symbolize heaven as a place of bounty. Five major themes are present in this passage: (1) the river of the water of life, (2) the tree of life, (3) God and the Lamb are the center and source of all, (4) God's children worship and share His reign forever, and (5) all evil fruit will be absent.[6]

The garden of Eden portrays an original creation in which God and human beings dwelt in harmony and bounty. When people sinned against God and were expelled from the garden, they were estranged from God and from each other. They lost sight of their destiny. Even the earth became hostile and under a curse.

When God's work of redemption shall be complete, heaven will be again like the garden of Eden. God will be in the center, the Creator and Giver of all. Human beings will live in harmonious relationship to God and with one another. God's will shall prevail.

Heaven Is Like Rest

After creating the world, the Bible says, "And on the seventh day God finished his work which he had done, and he rested on the seventh day from all his work which he had done. So God blessed the seventh day" (Gen. 2:2-3).

The sabbath was established on the basis of this seventh day of creation. It became a day of rest not only for human beings but also for the beasts of burden. Rest is a kind of celebration after meaningful toil.

The biblical narratives remind us that human life does consist of toil, travel, labor, and pilgrimage. The yearning for rest at the end of the week easily becomes the longing for rest at the end of a long journey. This longing extends to the hope for the rest of heaven at the end of life.

The author of Hebrews spoke of this presence with God as rest (Heb. 3:11, 18; 4:1, 3, 8-9). He viewed life as a pilgrimage and wrote, "So then, there remains a sabbath rest for the people of God; for whoever enters God's rest also ceases from his labors as God did from his" (4:9-10). Heaven will be like rest at the end of a long and difficult journey.

The figure of heaven as rest is also prominent in the Book of Revelation. "I heard a voice from heaven saying, 'Write this: Blessed are the dead who die in the Lord henceforth.' "Blessed indeed,' says the Spirit, 'that they may rest from their labors, for their deeds follow them!' " (14:13).

Rest is not the same as idleness or inactivity. This simile probably stresses celebration of victory. It may well include the worship of God and activities of great meaning.

Heaven Is Like a Victory

"But thanks be to God, who gives us the victory through our Lord Jesus Christ" (1 Cor. 15:57). In Revelation, John dramatizes the final and cosmic victory over evil. Human life is one of struggle. The conflict includes powers and principalities not of our making.

Throughout life we are encouraged to trust God and live godly lives in the world. We seek victory not in the sense of escape, but in the sense of reaching the goal with integrity in spite of the wounds.

In earthly history we point to great events as victories. Armistice Day was a day of victory we thought. The nations had laid down their weapons, but they had not beaten them into plowshares. In 1945 we had a VE-Day in Europe and a VJ-Day in the Pacific. These historic events in our time look less like victories now than they did in 1918 and 1945. Human victories appear often to have within them the seed of the next conflict. True victory always lies beyond.

Eternal life is a victory, total victory which will know no future conflict, have no regrets, and no lingering hostilities to breed more alienation. The way of war leaves casualties, hatreds, resentments, and boundary lines which occasion future wars. The way of the cross is the way of one casualty, Jesus Christ, and leaves no hatreds for the future. Heaven is a victory without mixture, pure victory.

Conclusion: With the Lord Always!

In the great passage in 1 Thessalonians 4:13-18, Paul gave a general view of the coming of Christ, the resurrection and eternal life. Paul concluded that those deceased and those still living will "be caught up together with them in the clouds to meet the Lord in the air; and so we shall always be with the Lord. Therefore comfort one another with these words" (vv. 17-18).

"So we shall always be with the Lord" is an adequate statement for heaven. Heaven is to be with the Lord. The pronoun "we" includes all of us who have believed in the Lord, both the living and the dead. This promise should be repeated for mutual encouragement.

If you have read this far, perhaps you will permit me to tell a rather personal story from my family. My wife and I had two sons and a daughter. Mark is my older son. Anna is my daughter. Jeorg was three and one-half years younger than Mark and died before Anna was born. Mark was about five when we lost his brother. Some months after our loss, Mark called me into his bedroom one night. I had thought that he was already asleep, but he had been lying in bed thinking about his younger brother. He said to me, "Will there be toys in heaven like little trucks and cars?" I gave him a lecture in theology, telling him that heaven is where God is, so everything will be right. He spoke reassuringly to me before he went to sleep, "Then there will be little trucks and cars in heaven, because little boys like Jeorg will not be happy without them."

We are all children. We look into the uncertain future with our hopes and fears. We may go astray if we project our human values into eternity. We may remain closer to the truth if we think of heaven as being with the Lord always. We should also "comfort one another with these words."

During the preparation of this manuscript I lost one of my lifelong friends, Dr. John E. Steely, a colleague on the faculty of my seminary. We met as college freshmen. About three months ago my oldest sister, Eunice Balfour, lost her struggle with cancer. It is obvious that the grief remaining from these losses has colored these pages. It is my belief that we shall all be reunited beyond death. I believe that after Christ's redeeming work in our lives has become complete, we shall have the capacity in heaven for loving everyone as much as we love those dearest to us in this life.

Perhaps we shall do no harm if we think of dying as lying down to sleep and the resurrection as awakening in heaven.

Let me conclude my witness with an intimate and personal story. My son Jeorg was only a year and a half old when he died. He could understand and talk in phrases. We had a ritual at bedtime. When we placed him in bed, pulled the covers over him, kissed him good night, we said something like, "We will see you in the morning." Jeorg's abbreviated response was "in the morning." Eleven days before his death he lapsed into a coma. The last words he said to me on that last night of consciousness were those words, "in the morning."

To you, who are believers and have read this book and have not met either me or one another, I pledge to you that we shall meet "in the morning!"

Notes

1. Baron Friedrich Von Hügel, *Eternal Life, a Study of Its Implications · and Applications* (Edinburgh: T & T. Clark, 1912), p. 64.

2. William Hendriksen, *The Bible on the Life Hereafter* (Grand Rapids: Baker Book House, 1959), pp. 208 *ff.*

3. C. Ryder Smith, *The Bible Doctrine of the Hereafter* (London: The Epworth Press, 1958), p. 236.

4. Ray Summers, *The Life Beyond* (Nashville: Broadman Press, 1959), pp. 204 *ff.*

5. Dale Moody, *The Word of Truth* (Grand Rapids: William B. Eerdmans Publishing Company, 1981), pp. 576-594.

6. Morris Ashcraft, "Revelation," *The Broadman Bible Commentary,* (Nashville: Broadman Press, 1972), 12:357.

Scripture Index